the beatles

every little thing

the beatles

every little thing

a compendium of witty, weird and ever-surprising facts about the fab four

MAXWELL MACKENZIE

AVON BOOKS NEW YORK

avon books, inc.

1350 Avenue of the Americas
New York, New York 10019

Library of Congress Cataloging in Publication Data:

MacKenzie, Maxwell.
The Beatles : every little thing / Maxwell MacKenzie.
p.   cm.
Includes bibliographic references (p. 210).
1. Beatles. 2. Rock musicians—England—Biography. I. Title.
ML421.B4M16   1998   98-28641
782.42166'092'2—dc21   CIP

First Avon Books Trade Paperback Printing: December 1998

AVON TRADEMARK REG. U.S. PAT. OFF. AND IN OTHER COUNTRIES, MARCA REGISTRADA,
HECHO EN U.S.A.

Printed in the U.S.A.

OPM   10 9 8 7 6 5 4 3 2 1

contents

the beatles

every little thing

dates, anniversaries, and events

July 7, 1940 .... Richard Starkey (Ringo Starr) born at home in Liverpool.

October 9, 1940 .... John Lennon born at the Oxford Street Maternity Home, Liverpool.

June 18, 1942 .... Paul McCartney born at Walton General Hospital, Liverpool.

February 25, 1943 .... George Harrison born at home in Wavertree, Liverpool.

July 6, 1957 .... John and Paul meet at St. Peter's, Woolton, Liverpool.

January 1960 .... Stuart Sutcliffe joins the band as bassist.

May 20–28, 1960 .... The Beatles' first tour, in Scotland, with Johnny Gentle.

February 9, 1961 .... The Beatles' first show at the Cavern.

November 9, 1961 .... Brian Epstein meets the Beatles.

January 24, 1962 .... The Beatles sign Epstein as manager.

June 6, 1962 .... The Beatles audition for Parlophone at Abbey Road.

August 16, 1962 .... Pete Best fired; Ringo joins the Beatles.

August 23, 1962 .... John Lennon and Cynthia Powell marry.

September 4, 1962 .... The Beatles record "Love Me Do" and "How Do You Do It," at Abbey Road Studios, London.

October 5, 1962 .... The Beatles' first single, "Love Me Do," released in the U.K. with "P.S. I Love You" (all release dates below are for the U.K.).

January 11, 1963 .... "Please Please Me" released with "Ask Me Why."

February 22, 1963 .... "Please Please Me" hits number one on the U.K. charts.

March 22, 1963.............. *Please Please Me* album released.

August 23, 1963............. "She Loves You" released with "I'll Get You."

October 14, 1963........... The term "Beatlemania" first used.

October 25–29, 1963..... First overseas tour, in Sweden.

November 22, 1963........ *With the Beatles* released.

January 18, 1964 .... "I Want to Hold Your Hand" enters the *Billboard* Hot 100.

February 7, 1964............ The Beatles fly to New York for their first U.S. concerts.

February 9, 1964............ First *Ed Sullivan Show* appearance.

June 4–June 30, 1964..... First world tour.

July 6, 1964..................... *A Hard Day's Night* premieres in London.

July 10, 1964................... *A Hard Day's Night* soundtrack released.

August 19–
   September 20, 1964.... First American tour.

August 28, 1964............. The Beatles first try marijuana.

December 4, 1964.......... *Beatles for Sale* released.

February 11, 1965 .... Ringo Starr and Maureen Cox married.

August 6, 1965............... *Help!* soundtrack released.

August 15–31, 1965 .... Second American tour.

October 26, 1965.............The Beatles made Members of the Order of the British Empire by Queen Elizabeth.

December 3, 1965.......... *Rubber Soul* released.

January 21, 1966 .... George Harrison and Patti Boyd married.

August 5, 1966............... *Revolver* released.

August 12–30, 1966 .... Final American tour.

November 9 or 10,
   1966........................... To many in the "Paul is Dead" cult, the date Paul was killed in a car crash.

June 1, 1967................... *Sgt. Pepper's Lonely Hearts Club Band* released.

August 24, 1967............. The Beatles meet Maharishi Mahesh Yogi in London.

August 26, 1967............. Brian Epstein found dead.

December 8, 1967.......... *Magical Mystery Tour* EP released.

February 1968 .... Beatles fly to India for the Maharishi's three-month meditation course.

October 18, 1968 .... John and Yoko arrested for possession of cannabis.

November 22, 1968 .... *The Beatles* (a.k.a. "the White Album") released.

January 17, 1969 .... *Yellow Submarine* soundtrack released.

March 12, 1969 .... Paul and Linda Eastman married. George and Patti Harrison's house raided by narcotics officers.

May 20, 1969 .... Allen Klein signed as manager to the Beatles. Paul refuses to sign the contract.

September 26, 1969 .... *Abbey Road* released.

November 8, 1969 .... John and Cynthia's divorce finalized.

January 4, 1970 .... Paul, Ringo, and George finish their overdubs for the *Let It Be* album, the last occasion they would have to record for the band. John was on vacation.

April 10, 1970 .... Paul announces that he is leaving the Beatles.

May 8, 1970 .... *Let It Be* released.

December 31, 1970 .... Paul sues the other three Beatles to dissolve their partnership.

December 8, 1980 .... John Lennon murdered in New York.

names

john, born during a German bombing raid in Liverpool in 1940, was given the patriotic middle name Winston, after Britain's leader and wartime inspiration.

paul, born to a Catholic mother and Anglican-born but agnostic father, was named James Paul McCartney. "James" was the name of his father, great-grandfather, and great-great-grandfather, and the "Paul" was a tribute to St. Paul. Paul would, in turn, name his son James.

ringo Starr was born Richard Starkey to Elsie and Richard Starkey, and became known as Little Richard, while his dad was called Big Richard. Ringo's grandfather's last name was originally Parkin, but he changed it to Starkey. By the time Little Richard was five, he was known simply as Ritchie. When he was playing with Rory Storm and the Hurricanes, Rory renamed Ritchie "Ringo Starr" and introduced "Ringo Starrtime" into his act, where Ringo would sing "Boys" and "You're Sixteen."

john's first band received the name The Quarry Men, a reference to both the Liverpool quarries and the Quarry Bank Grammar School. They covered skiffle classics such as "Rock

Island Line," "Worried Man Blues," and "Long Black Train," as well as rock 'n' roll numbers such as "Blue Suede Shoes."

after George came to the band, the name Quarry Men was dropped and the band tried such names as the Rainbows, or the Moondogs, or, for one night, Johnny and the Moondogs. When, in April 1960, John and Paul performed together for an engagement at a pub, they went by the name the Nerk Twins.

facing another audition in 1959, the band began searching for a new name. John had been listening to Buddy Holly and the Crickets, and explained to Hunter Davies, the "official" Beatles biographer, "I was sitting at home one day, just thinking about what a good name the Crickets would be for an English group. The idea of beetles came into my head. I decided to spell it Beatles to make it look like beat music, just as a joke." A friend of theirs thought the name was horrible, and suggested "Long John and the Silver Beatles," insisting that bands had to have long names. "Silver Beatles" thus became their name for the remainder of 1959. In 1960 they experimented with "The Beatals," "The Silver Beats," and "Silver Beetles."

another account has the name coming from Stuart, who suggested it without the "a" spelling. When John wrote a comic history of the group for *Mersey Beat* in 1961, he said, "It came in a vision—a man appeared on a flaming pie and said unto them 'From this day on you are Beatles with an A.' Thank you, Mister Man, they said, thanking him."

when working on the *Anthology* series, the surviving Beatles also looked into the idea that John and Stu had been inspired by the classic Marlon Brando film *The Wild One*. In the film, which was a favorite of John's, the Lee Marvin character, "Chino," refers to the girls in the gang as "beetles."

for their first tour, Paul adopted the stage name "Paul Ramon," while George came up with "Carl Harrison," after Carl Perkins. Stuart Sutcliffe adopted the name of a contemporary artist, "Stuart DeStael," and John went as "Johnny Silver."

in June 1969, John changed his middle name, dropping "Winston" for "John Ono Lennon." Yoko became Yoko Ono Lennon.

yoko Ono's name means "ocean child."

places

on the day John's parents, Freddy Lennon and Julia Stanley, married, they met on the steps of the Adelphi Hotel in Liverpool. The hotel, now the Britannia Adelphi, is today the site of an annual Beatles convention each August.

john was raised by his aunt Mimi at "Mendips," at 251 Menlove Avenue, a small house in a suburb three miles northeast of Liverpool known as Woolton. His first school, which he entered at the age of four, was Dovetail Primary School.

george, three grades behind John, also attended Dovetail, but they never met. George later moved on to the Liverpool Institute in 1954, where Paul was a student one year ahead of him.

george stood out at Liverpool Institute, and Paul remembers him for having long hair and extravagant dress. He tightened his pants and snuck a bright yellow waistcoat under his school uniform. However, his rebellion didn't go far beyond dress: "I learned it was best to keep cool and shut up. I had this mutual thing with a few masters. They'd let me sleep at the back and I wouldn't cause any trouble."

george finally met Paul on their shared bus route. They hung out sporadically, and practiced guitar at George's place.

paul says he loved riding the two-decker buses in Liverpool, and always rode upstairs, where smoking was permitted and he had a view of the streets. He says also that these memories came out in the "A Day in the Life" line about smoking upstairs and drifting off into a dream. The bus also figures, of course, in "Penny Lane," the main transfer point for Liverpool buses.

john found early musical expression in the choir at St. Peter's Parish Church, Woolton, where he was later confirmed. Still later, St. Peter's became the site of some of John's earliest gigs with his first band, the Quarry Men, during the church's youth club "hops." It was during one of these church events, an outdoor summer party, where Paul first saw John's band perform. They met later that day in the church hall.

at the age of twelve, John started at Quarry Bank Grammar School, where he met lifelong friend Pete Shotton. John evidently did not excel at Quarry Bank. One of John's reports from school read, "Hopeless. Rather a clown in class. A shocking report. He is just wasting other pupils' time." Another read, "Certainly on the road to failure." He wound up in the lowest track—the "C stream," with the "thick lads." He later failed his O levels (exams given to "Ordinary" students), and might not have made it into Liverpool College of Art if he hadn't been helped by his headmaster.

⚓

paul, on the other hand, in his years at primary school at Stockton Road Primary and later at Joseph Williams Primary, was composed and studious, easily earning top marks in most lessons, particularly English and art. He even received a 90 percent in Latin.

⚓

through Paul's exemplary academic performance, he was offered a place at the city's oldest grammar school, Liverpool Institute, which was located in the same structure as Liverpool College of Art, where John would later become a student.

⚓

on a last day before break at the Institute, Paul brought his guitar to class, stood on a desk, and played and sang two Little Richard songs: "Long Tall Sally" and "Tutti Frutti."

⚓

ringo received the least education of the four Beatles, as he suffered a series of childhood illnesses and spent a good deal of his time in hospitals.

paul's family first settled in the suburb of Anfield, close to the burial grounds of numerous victims of the blitz. The family moved to a rent-free council estate in Speke when Paul was four. When Paul was thirteen, his family moved closer to the center of Liverpool, to a council house in the cleaner district of Allerton.

although Speke was a rough and dirty district, it was on the far outskirts of Liverpool, and offered Paul peaceful woods, streams, and rivers nearby. The time he spent there, he says, is what he was singing about in "Mother Nature's Son."

george's family also lived in a Speke council house, at 25 Upton Green. They moved there when George was six, after the family had been on the waiting list for eighteen years.

early influences

john's mother, Julia, received lessons on the banjo from her husband before he left her, in the same year John was born. When John formed his first band, the Quarry Men, they often practiced at Julia's house, and she would help by teaching them chords on her banjo.

after the Beatles became household names, John's dad, Freddy Lennon, resurfaced for a meeting with John. It didn't go as well as he had hoped, and the next time he knocked on John's door, he was abruptly dismissed. He did paid interviews for *Tid Bits* and *Weekend* magazine, and later had a record release, "That's My Life."

john's favorite schoolboy songs were "Let Him Go, Let Him Tarry," and "Wee Willie Winkie."

paul auditioned for choir at the Anglican Cathedral, Liverpool, the largest Anglican cathedral in Europe, in 1953, but was turned down.

at age seven, John's favorite books were *Alice in Wonderland* and *The Wind in the Willows*. He also loved the Just William stories, and says he wrote some William stories himself and poems which recalled "Jabberwocky." The Lewis Carroll influence is apparent in songs such as "I Am the Walrus" and "Lucy in the Sky with Diamonds."

john appeared to be a mystic even at an early age. When he was not yet ten, he declared to his family that he had been talking to God, who was enjoying the heat from their fire.

john's aunt Mimi considered sending John to music lessons, but he objected to the structure of *any* sort of lesson, so the idea was shelved. However, at age ten, John became friendly with a bus conductor who played a mouth organ on his route. The conductor liked John and bought him a new mouth organ. Mimi says this was the "first encouragement he ever had."

john first heard Elvis Presley's "Heartbreak Hotel" in 1956, and he immediately became a huge fan of the singer. Late at night, he would tune into Radio Luxembourg (since the BBC did not play rock 'n' roll) to absorb the sounds of Elvis, Little Richard, and Bill Haley. Soon, he also became infatuated with the newly arrived "skiffle" bands, which used home-made instruments such as tin cans and washboards, as well as banjos and guitars. They covered American folk, jazz, and blues songs, and skiffle quickly became a national craze. John began annoying

Julia and Mimi for the money to buy a guitar, until finally his aunt gave in and took him to the local music shop to purchase a secondhand Spanish guitar with steel strings, marked "Guaranteed not to Split."

at the same time, although they had not met, Paul was receiving inspiration from the rock 'n' roll of Elvis, Little Richard, and Carl Perkins, and attempted to learn their guitar solos. He especially favored Elvis's "All Shook Up" and attempted to emulate that single's guitar solos on his instrument. He also liked the sounds of the Everly Brothers, a more harmonious American duo whose neat matching fashions were copied by Paul and his friends.

paul's first attempt to form a band with his younger brother, Michael, on banjo was directly inspired by the Everly Brothers. The attempt was short-lived, however, as Michael broke his arm at Boy Scout camp.

the focus of Paul and John's musical inspiration was above all black American music. According to Paul: "That's what we used to listen to, what we used to like and what we wanted to be like. . . . Whenever we were asked who our favorite people were, we'd say, 'Black, R&B, Motown.' "

ringo played with a skiffle band as a teenager, the Eddie Clayton Skiffle Group, made up of his co-workers (he was working as a fitter). His stepfather presented him with a secondhand drum set, which he played regularly for the Darktown Skiffle Group and irregularly for other bands. He joined Al Caldwell's Texans in 1959, which soon was renamed Rory Storm & the Hurricanes. This band's gigs at the Cavern made them the most popular band in Merseyside by 1960.

by the time the Beatles asked him to join, Ringo was well on his way to supporting himself through drumming. He had received an offer to work in Hamburg with Tony Sheridan which included a flat, a car, and £30 a week. When he declined and returned to Liverpool to play with Rory, he soon received two offers: "I got another offer at the same time, from King Size and the Dominoes. He offered £20 a week [about $370 in 1997 U.S. dollars]. The Beatles offered £25, so I took them."

in the 1920s, Paul's father, Jim McCartney, who was self-taught on piano, formed the Jim Mac Jazz Band with family members and played at local dances and parties around Liverpool. One of the band's jobs was adding the live score to a silent Hollywood film, *The Queen of Sheba*.

paul's grandfather played an E-flat bass for his company brass band. Paul holds an E-flat bass on an early sketch of the cover of *Sgt. Pepper's Lonely Hearts Club Band*.

paul received a trumpet as a gift when he was fourteen, and taught himself a few tunes. He later traded his trumpet for a £15 (about $240 in 1997 U.S. dollars) Zenith Guitar when he realized he couldn't sing and play trumpet at the same time.

The guitar was worth just less than two weeks' worth of his father's 1956 wages.

paul's father kept an upright piano in the home, and Paul learned how to play by ear, even though he made at least two attempts at formal lessons.

Coincidentally, the piano was bought from Brian Epstein's family business, North End Music Stores (NEMS).

when he was fourteen, George started to become fascinated with guitars, and talked his father into buying him one, secondhand, for three pounds (around $47 in 1997 U.S. dollars). Although it sat in a closet for three months, when he picked it up again, his mother encouraged him until he had grown beyond what she could teach him. His parents then sprang for a £30 electric guitar, which might have seemed a real extravagance. George's dad had gone through the Depression and spent fifteen months making only 23 shillings (£1.15) a week on the dole.

george quickly got a band together—with his brother Peter and his friend Arthur Kelly—when he secured an audition for a performance at the Speke British Legion. No other bands showed up for the audition, so George's went on to perform. They called themselves the Rebels and received ten shillings (about $5 in 1997 U.S. dollars) each.

george's parents remained supportive as the Beatles' popularity grew. But while George's mother was very encouraging, even showing up to some of the Cavern performances, Mimi was upset with where John's life was leading him. She showed up one night at the Cavern, barged past the doorman, and tried to get up to the stage with the plan of pulling John off. Unable to get through the crowd, she waited in the dressing room to tell him that he was returning to art college the next day. To Mrs. Harrison, she once said, "We'd all have had lovely peaceful lives but for you encouraging them."

years later, Mimi would accompany the Beatles on their Far East/Australia tour. She received adulation from the fans in Hong Kong as well, and the police opened a path for her by yelling, "John Mama, John Mama." She went home, shaken, after witnessing the huge crowds at Adelaide.

john may not have excelled at the art college, but he did find new role models and influences through his studies. He was especially fascinated with the "tortured genius" types:

"Oscar Wilde or Dylan Thomas or Vincent Van Gogh—the suffering they went through because of their vision. They were *seeing* and being tortured by society for trying to express . . . that loneliness and seeing what *is*."

john and Paul both suffered tragedies at an early age. John's father left him before he was born; his uncle, with whom he lived, died when John was twelve; and his mother died when he was seventeen, hit by a car right outside his aunt Mimi's house.

In 1955, when Paul was fourteen, Paul's mother began to notice a pain in her breast, but did not seek medical attention. When the pain became so severe that she did consult a physician, she was diagnosed with breast cancer. When the doctors initiated a mastectomy operation, they discovered that the cancer had progressed too far to be cured; a few hours later, she died. Paul's immediate response to the news of his mother's death was shocking in itself: "What are we going to do without her money?" But he also says this was a reaction of concern for the welfare of the family, and that he cried and prayed for her return.

ringo, like John, came from a broken home. His father and mother were divorced in 1943, and Ringo joined his mother. She married again ten years later.

only George grew up with both of his natural parents.

by 1956, Britain had endured a number of fundamental changes to its political, moral, and social structure, and one of these was the increasing rebelliousness of its teenagers, more and more of whom embraced an outrageous sense of style and attitude. They were known as "Teddy Boys" because of the Edwardian fashions they imitated: they wore ruffled shirts and tapered trousers, velvet-piped jackets, brightly-colored socks and thick-soled shoes, with hair slicked on either side into what would become known as a ducktail. According to the headmaster of Liverpool's Quarry Bank Grammar School, two of his charges, John Lennon and Pete Shotton, were the worst Teds of the school. They had learned to dress the part while playing truant, by watching the merchant seamen at the docks on leave. Although John was forbidden by his aunt Mimi from wearing Teddy Boy clothes to school, he would leave home dressed to suit her approval and change into his preferred style at Julia's house, and his mother would sometimes buy him the very clothes her sister had forbidden.

at about the same time, Paul's father began to notice Paul's transformation into a Teddy Boy, which he vigorously discouraged.

in 1956, Paul saw Lonnie Donegan and his skiffle group at Liverpool's Empire Theater. Soon afterwards, Paul acquired his first guitar, which he had limited success at until he saw a picture of the left-handed guitar player Slim Whitman, and realized that his guitar was for a right-handed player. He restrung the guitar backward, using a wooden match to keep the smallest string in the largest notch.

paul still owns this first guitar.

when he and John started practicing together, John, who mostly knew chords for the banjo, had to reverse Paul's left-handed fingering before he could play the guitar himself. He often had to practice in front of a mirror until he had it right.

john and Paul were introduced by a mutual friend, Ivan Vaughan, who invited Paul to watch John's skiffle group perform at a summer party at St. Peter's in Woolton. Paul brought his guitar, and played for John hits by Eddie Cochran, Gene Vincent, and Little Richard, some of which, like "Long Tall Sally," the Beatles would later record. A week later, Paul was approached by another Quarry Man, Pete Shotton, who told him that John wanted him in the band.

paul was the first to write an original tune, which he played for John. John was not to be left behind and started writing songs himself, which set a pattern for songwriting competitiveness that would direct the Beatles for years to come.

john and Paul wrote songs together in a notebook, heading each page with the notice, "Another Lennon–McCartney Original." They wrote a number of songs together before coming up with "Love Me Do," the first song from their early days that they actually went on to record.

the pair showed a great determination to learn their instruments. They once learned of a musician who knew the B7 chord, and took the bus from one side of town to the other to find him.

george was introduced to the Quarry Men by Paul and became accepted into the group by the much-older John. The band could now practice at George's and Paul's, but never at John's. Mimi wouldn't even let George in the house after he showed up with a crew cut and a pink shirt.

george's main selling point for his entry into the Quarry Men was that he could play solos. His first "audition" was a performance of Bill Justis's "Raunchy," which he played on the upstairs section of a Liverpool bus.

the Quarry Men made a one-off private recording on a shellac record of "That'll Be the Day" by Buddy Holly in

1958. This rarity has been found on bootleg tapes, but was never officially released.

stuart Sutcliffe, the best-known "fifth Beatle," met John at the Liverpool College of Art. Stu was often praised by his professors as the best artist to have attended the college. He was also deeply interested in beat poetry from San Francisco, mystic philosophy, and the films of Andrzej Wajda. When he won sixty pounds in an art competition, he bought a bass guitar so he could join the group. The other members taught him how to play.

a few firsts

paul wrote his first song, "I Lost My Little Girl," when he was fourteen, shortly after his mother died.

as Paul remembers it, his first collaboration with John was on a song called "Too Bad About Sorrows."

perhaps the earliest press photograph of John was taken in July 1960 for *People,* a national British tabloid. John appears in a photo of a group of youths with the headline "The Beatnik Horror, for though they don't know it they are on the road to hell."

the Quarry Men made their first appearance at the Cavern Club in August 1957. Paul was not able to make this performance; his first appearance with them would be at a gig at the Conservative Club in Norris Green, Liverpool, on October 18, 1957. The Beatles made their first Cavern Club appearance in February 1961, during a lunchtime session. On March 21, 1961, they made their first evening appearance at the club. By the time of their last Cavern show, on August 3, 1961, they had made between 275 and 290 appearances, and earned £300 (almost $4,500 in 1997 U.S. dollars) for their last gig.

After the madness of the Beatles' last tour, John pleaded with Brian Epstein to let them go back to simpler times at the Cavern Club: "Couldn't we do a few numbers down there, just for old times' sake?" Epstein replied that if they attempted it, the band would be literally crushed.

the Quarry Men's first performing "gear" was purchased soon after Paul joined. These outfits included fringed white cowboy shirts, black bolo ties, and black pants. John and Paul, now the two leads, also wore white blazers.

the Beatles' first tour took them to Scotland as an opening act for Johnny Gentle. When they auditioned for Larry Parnes, who had discovered Tommy Steele in 1956, their drummer failed to show, and the role was filled by a middle-aged Johnny Hutch, who was a much seasoned musician than any of the Beatles. They were picked for the two-week tour, and got an unemployed drummer named Thomas Moore to join them.

the Beatles' first long-term engagement, before Hamburg and the Cavern Club, was at the Casbah Club, run by John and Mona Best, parents of drummer Pete Best, out of the basement of their large Victorian House at 8 Haymans Green, West Derby, Liverpool. Still known as the Quarry Men, they briefly served as resident band in 1959, and John and Cynthia had helped with the decoration. Pete Best joined the Beatles as drummer when they were offered a residence in Hamburg.

mona Best also became the band's first active manager, securing gigs at St. John's Hall, Tuebrook, and attempting to get them on local television. When they returned from Hamburg, Mona hyped them with posters reading "The Return of the Fabulous Beatles," and they started another long engagement.

the first Beatles riot happened shortly after they returned from Hamburg at the Litherland Town Hall, where they played with a few other local bands: on December 27, 1960. The Beatles, still relatively unknown locally, received the billing, "Direct from Hamburg." Their performance provoked a minor riot, and a series of decent club bookings came right out of this performance, causing several commentators to name this performance as a major turning point in the band's development.

the Beatles first encountered Ringo Starr at the Kaiserkeller in Hamburg, where a number of English bands had secured gigs. Ringo was drumming for Rory Storm and the Hurricanes. George remembered seeing Ringo at the club: "I didn't like the look of Rory's drummer myself. He looked the nasty one, with this little gray streak of hair. But the nastier one turned out to be Ringo, the nicest of them all."

the Beatles first played with Ringo on October 15, 1960, at a small "vanity" studio that catered to Hamburg visitors who wanted to record their voice for friends back home. Ringo stood in for Pete as the Beatles backed up Lu Walters of the Hurricanes on "Summertime," "Fever," and "September Song."

ringo's first public performance with the Beatles was on August 18, 1962, at Hulme Hall, Liverpool.

during the band's second trip to Germany in April 1961, they made their first professional studio visit. A local promoter hired them as the "Beat Brothers" to back up Tony Sheridan on "When the Saints Go Marching In," "My Bonnie Lies Over the Ocean," "Why (Can't You Love Me Again)," "Sweet Georgia Brown," "Nobody's Child," and "If You Love Me Baby." They also recorded "Ain't She Sweet," a song from the twenties, written by Jack Yellen and Milton Ager, and recorded by Gene Vincent. This was the one song which left Sheridan in the background, with John singing lead vocals. George came up with an instrumental number taking off on the band the Shadows, called "Cry for a Shadow." The "Beat Brothers" were paid twenty-six pounds (almost $400 U.S. 1997) for their time.

the Beatles won their first *Mersey Beat* readers' poll for best Liverpool band in December 1961.

according to Brian Epstein's autobiography and Hunter Davies's authorized Beatles biography, Epstein first heard the name "Beatles" on October 28, 1961, while working at his record store. A young man asked if he had a record by them called "My Bonnie." This was the record they had recorded in Germany under a different name, so Brian, who had built the business on his wide stock and ability to get any record, was stumped. The following Monday, two more customers asked for the record, and Brian began to make inquiries.

Brian first saw the Beatles perform at the Cavern on November 9, 1961, and met the band. It turned out that they were all visitors of his store, and that Epstein had been tempted to toss them out for their rough appearances and scanty purchases. When he found out from George that their record was on Polydor, he was able to place an order for two hundred copies.

Several commentators, however, have questioned whether this account is accurate. The Beatles were in nearly every issue of *Mersey Beat,* the local music magazine that Epstein not only carried in his store, but wrote columns for. Their pictures were in the magazine, and he easily might have recognized them during their visits.

the Beatles first appeared at Abbey Road on June 6, 1962, for an audition. Those who recall the audition agree that it was the personalities, humor, and stage presence of the Beatles, rather than their musical ability, that got them signed. According to George Martin: "The material didn't impress me, least of all their own songs. I felt that I was going to have to find suitable material for them, and was quite certain that their songwriting ability had no salable future!" However, their humor, coupled with enthusiasm and professionalism, brought them a contract.

One example of Beatle humor mentioned by George Martin was George Harrison's comment after he had given them a lecture about what technical points they needed to work on. To put them back at ease, he asked them if there was anything they didn't like. "Yeah, I don't like your tie," replied Harrison.

the Beatles themselves, along with Brian Epstein, believed that they were at Abbey Road to record, not to audition. George Martin had sent Brian a contract, but had not countersigned it, and did not plan to do so unless he liked the band live.

They placed four songs on tape during the two-hour audition: "Love Me Do," "P.S. I Love You," "Ask Me Why," and Paul's version of "Bésame Mucho."

the first recording the Beatles did specifically for an EMI single, on September 4, 1962, was a version of "How Do You Do It," which was a song requested by George Martin. The Beatles' version was not released, but their arrangement was picked up by Gerry and the Pacemakers, who turned it into a number one hit.

"love Me Do," the Beatles' first single on Parlophone, was released on October 5, 1962. On October 24, it reached number 27 on the U.K. charts, but fell off in the next week and didn't appear again until December 27, when it reached number 17.

the next single was the first Beatles single to reach number one in the U.K. charts. "Please Please Me" was released on January 11, 1963, and found a place on the charts on January 30. It hit number one on February 22, and stayed at the top for two weeks.

the Beatles' first television appearance came shortly after their first record release, on *People and Places,* out of Manchester and only shown in the north of England.

george Harrison's first solo composition, other than his Shadows parody, "Cry for a Shadow," was "Don't Bother Me," which appeared on the album *With the Beatles*.

recorded from February 25 to March 1, 1964, *A Hard Day's Night* was the first and only Beatles album to consist entirely of songs written by Lennon/McCartney. However, the version released in the United States contained the seven songs used in the soundtrack of the film, four orchestrations of Beatles songs arranged by George Martin, and "I'll Cry

Instead," which was cut from the film. The version of this last song on the United States album contains an extra verse.

they received their first write-up in a national paper when Maureen Cleave wrote a general feature for the *Evening Standard* in February 1963. She described their sense of humor and called their haircuts "French style." Maureen Cleave would later be the reporter who printed John's comments about Christ, which caused a furor in the United States.

in February 1963 the band embarked on their first national tour, with Helen Shapiro headlining. The promoter, Arthur Howes, would go on to manage all but one of the Beatles' British tours. It was while they were on the Helen Shapiro tour that "Please Please Me" reached number one. The tour lasted from February 2 to March 3, 1963, and included fourteen stops. Also performing were Danny Williams, Kenny Lynch, the Honeys, the Kestrels, and the Red Price Band. Dave Allen acted as compere. Six days after this tour was completed, they left on another, setting a pattern which would eventually leave them exhausted.

the Beatles' first radio appearance was on the BBC show "Teenager's Turn." They recorded "Dream Baby" for the March 8, 1962, broadcast.

the Beatles' first overseas tour was in Sweden, where they played a show a night from October 25 to 29, 1963.

"i Want to Hold Your Hand" was the Beatles' first song to break the American Top 40; released in the United States on January 13, 1964, it entered the Hot 100 on January 18, 1964, made the Top 40 on January 25, and stayed there for fourteen weeks.

the Beatles' first United States concert was held at the Washington Coliseum in Washington, D.C., on February 11, 1964, where they performed on a rotating stage.

the Beatles' first world tour lasted from June 4 to June 30, 1964, with seventeen stops in Denmark, Hong Kong, Australia, and New Zealand.

"can't Buy Me Love" was the first Beatles single to go straight to number one in the States. When it did, the Beatles broke all previous records for U.S. chart dominance. The April 4, 1964, chart shows the Beatles in twelve spots, including one through five with "Can't Buy Me Love," "Twist and Shout," "She Loves You," "I Want to Hold Your Hand," and "Please Please Me." Meanwhile, *Meet the Beatles* and *Introducing the Beatles* held the top two spots on the album charts.

"**can't** Buy Me Love" was also the first single ever to go straight to number one on both the U.S. and U.K. charts.

although it may be fairly common now for megastar musicians to see advance orders for albums in excess of a million copies, it happened first with the Beatles' *Help!*, released in the U.S. on August 13, 1965. Advance orders in the United States alone, where the album was at number one for nine weeks, were enough to give the Beatles a gold record even before it went on sale.

early gigs, clubs, and auditions

after George joined up with John and Paul, the band's emphasis shifted from gigs to talent competitions, which they usually lost, once to a woman who played spoons.

another disappointment came in 1959, when "Mr. Star Maker, Carroll Levis" held auditions in Liverpool for his television show, *Carroll Levis Discoveries,* which ran out of Manchester. The trio made the audition and they were invited to Manchester, but had to leave on the last train before they finished the competition.

in Liverpool, the band spends several nights at a strip bar on Upper Parliament Street, backing up the resident stripper, "Janice," with songs like "Ramrod" and "Moonglow."

in 1960 the Beatles secured a residence at the Indra and later the Kaiserkeller, both clubs in Hamburg, a northern German port town. The club was located in the seedy Reeperbahn district, an area full of strip clubs like the Indra that catered to gangsters and foreign sailors. Pete Best recalled the five months in Hamburg as a major influence on the band's development: "We'd been meek and mild musicians at first, now we became a powerhouse."

Other Liverpool bands in Hamburg actually tried to block the Beatles from coming, thinking that this untried group would give the others a bad name.

They were given sleeping quarters in a run-down old cinema, and paid two and a half pounds per day, each (roughly equal to thirty-eight 1997 U.S. dollars). Paul's father, by comparison, was earning eight pounds a week in 1956 as a cotton salesman, and George's father's first job paid just over half a pound per week.

they attempted a German song only once—"Wooden Heart," which was then a minor hit.

the environment in the clubs was one of impending violence, and often actual violence. The waiters at the Kaiserkeller were all ex-boxers, who wielded spring-loaded truncheons and had tear gas readily available to clear the club if necessary. Nonetheless, John would often shout insults in English at the crowd or, as he relates, "Call them Nazis and tell them to fuck off." Luckily for them, most patrons didn't speak English, and would respond with cheers.

the Hamburg adventure came to a sudden end when the band attempted to leave the Kaiserkeller for a more upscale club. George was deported for being underage (he was seventeen) and without work papers. Then, after a performance, Paul and Pete Best were accused of starting a fire at the

Bambi. They had fastened four condoms to the wall and set them on fire to provide light while they packed their things, leaving burn marks on the wall. They were arrested and deported. John and Stuart's work permits were soon taken away, and they returned to Liverpool in December 1960, after four months in Hamburg.

after Hamburg, the band played a series of ballroom gigs, many of which ended in riots, not all innocent. Paul told Beatle biographer Hunter Davies, "At the Grosvenor Ballroom in Wallasey there would be a hundred Wallasey lads all ready to fight a hundred lads from Secombe when things got going. . . . The Hambledon Hall was another place where there was often fights. They used fire extinguishers on each other one night there."

their next serious long-term engagement was at the Cavern Club, where they played regularly for over two years. During their stay, they appeared on bills with several notable musicians, such as Johnny Sandon and the Searchers, Gene Vincent, Billy J. Kramer, the Coasters, Simone Jackson, and Little Richard.

they returned to Hamburg as much more seasoned musicians in April 1961. They arrived by train this time, and had the proper work permits, sorted out for them by the club owner. Their contract demanded that they play every day of the week, from seven at night until two in the morning, but three in the morning on Saturdays. They stayed until July.

for their third visit to Hamburg, in April 1962, the still-unsigned band was able to afford their first plane trip.

hamburg was also their third stop on the 1966 Germany–Japan tour. At the Ernst Merck Halle, where they performed, 500 riot police gathered outside and used water cannons for crowd control. On the same tour, they were given use of the train used by Queen Elizabeth on her tour of Germany in 1965.

GETTING SIGNED

in May 1962, a chain of events brought the Beatles to a contract. Epstein took his tapes of the Beatles to London, and walked into the HMV record store on Oxford Street to ask how much it would cost to transfer them to vinyl. The technician on this job thought that music publisher Syd Coleman, whose office was upstairs, should hear them. Coleman in turn made an appointment for the very next day between Epstein and George Martin at Parlophone, a subsidiary of EMI. Although EMI had already turned the Beatles down, Martin had not been part of that decision.

martin's original favorite was the Beatles' version of "Till There Was You." He also liked Paul's singing on "Hello Little Girl." He invited them in for an audition.

in July 1962, George Martin finally contacted Brian with the news that he was interested in signing a contract. At the time, Parlophone had no runaway sales, and no pop artists. Although George Martin pioneered comedy recordings—including recordings with Peter Sellers—and worked with jazz artists like Stan Getz, he realized that he would have to sign a band with youth appeal to keep Parlophone running. This brought the Beatles to his studio.

Martin admits that he wasn't extremely impressed with the tapes he first heard, and envisioned the Beatles as a back-up band for a front man which he was sure to find eventually. "When I met them," he recalled, "I soon realized that would never work."

missed opportunities

john's good friend Pete Shotton left the Quarry Men after a gig at a party when John broke Pete Best's washboard over his head. Ivan Vaughan had left the group earlier, but was still friends with both Paul and John. These departures opened the way for George Harrison to come into the picture.

another of the many who would miss out on the chance to be a Beatle was bass player Chas Newby, who played with them when Stuart Sutcliffe was either still in Hamburg or recovering from tonsillitis. Chas, formerly with the Blackjacks, would play four gigs before returning to college.

allan Williams was the band's first professional manager, who secured for them the Johnny Gentle tour and their first engagement in Hamburg. After they secured their second Hamburg contract without Williams's help, they wrote to inform him that they intended to withhold his share from this particular arrangement. Williams threatened to sue, and later told Epstein to "not touch [the Beatles] with a ten-foot barge pole." Williams titled his autobiography *The Man Who Gave the Beatles Away.*

little Richard said that Brian Epstein offered him fifty percent of the management contract if he could get the Beatles an American studio. He refused, not wanting to get into the management business and thinking that the band would never make it. He claims, however, that he sent masters of their tapes to Vee Jay Records, who released them in the States when Capitol refused.

one of the most mysterious episodes in the history of the Beatles is the sacking of Pete Best as drummer. At one point, he was the most popular Beatle among Liverpool fans. Pete projected a melancholy air by playing drums with his head down, and had developed a playing style in Hamburg that depended heavily on the bass drum, giving a "big" sound. He eventually became so popular that for a Valentine's Day dance in 1961 his drum kit was placed in the front of the stage. The experiment was not repeated, because love-crazed girls mobbed him and pulled him off stage.

Pete Best was fired on August 16, 1962. Brian Epstein broke the news. To Pete, it came out of the blue: "He said, 'I've got some bad news for you. The boys want you out and Ringo in.' It was a complete bombshell. I was stunned. I couldn't say anything for two minutes."

Mersey Beat ran a cover story on the change in their next issue. The numerous fans of Pete Best sent hundreds of letters of protest to the magazine, picketed Epstein's music store, and even gave George Harrison a black eye. Brian Epstein became afraid to go near the Cavern, and hired a bodyguard.

While Brian offered to get Pete a position with the Mersey-beats, another Liverpool act, Pete declined, not wanting to work with Epstein. However, it was Epstein who quietly pulled strings to get an offer for Pete from Lee Curtis & the All Stars, which he accepted. He joined them in Hamburg, where they performed at the Star Club. In 1963 Lee Curtis left the band, which then became the Pete Best All Stars. They cut a single with Decca, "I'm Gonna Knock On Your Door," released in June 1964. Its sales failed to impress Decca, and they were dropped. After a suicide attempt and a failed attempt to break into the North American market, Pete eventually became a civil servant.

including Ringo, there have been at least five drummers for the Beatles. Norman Chapman was the drummer for the Silver Beatles for three weeks before leaving for military service. Tommy Moore was also drummer for about one month in 1960. Jimmy Nichol was a fill-in drummer for ten days in 1964, while the band was on their first world tour and Ringo was ill.

shortly after being signed as manager, Epstein got an artists and repertoire (A&R) representative from Decca to visit Liverpool and the Cavern to watch a Beatles performance, in late December 1961. The A&R man, Mike Smith, was impressed, and set up an audition for January 1, 1962.

For the Decca audition, George sang "The Sheik of Araby," and Paul sang "Red Sails in the Sunset" and "Like Dreamers Do." They were all terribly nervous, and after receiving compliments on the demo they had just made, were shown the door.

Paul said that this audition was the only time they let Epstein have a say in what they would perform. Much later, at Abbey Road, Brian made the mistake of commenting on their studio performance, and was quickly put in his place by John:

"You stick with your percentages, Brian. We'll look after the music."

Weeks later, Brian was told that Decca didn't like the Beatles' rough edges, and that there was no future in guitar-based bands. Electric guitars were "old hat." Brian then went knocking at EMI and Pye, along with smaller companies, and received similar answers.

In a later interview, Paul stated the obvious fact that Decca's A&R chief "must be kicking himself now," to which John added the comment, "I hope he kicks himself to death."

brian Epstein made a trip to the States in November 1963, traveling with Billy J. Kramer, to attempt to break the Beatles into the initially resistant U.S. music scene. It was on this trip that he finally persuaded Capitol Records, a subsidiary of EMI, to pick up the band. Their first singles had been released by smaller companies for U.S. distribution.

Incredibly, Capitol refused to take the Beatles at any price on three different occasions, after hearing three different singles. They were finally pressured by their parent company to take "I Want to Hold Your Hand." Later, they continued to turn down successful acts who later went on to success in the United States, such as the Dave Clark Five, the Animals, Herman's Hermits, the Hollies, Gerry and the Pacemakers, and the Yardbirds.

sid Bernstein, an agent for General Artists Corporation who had an interest in British Newspapers, was the first promoter to contact Epstein about a Beatles concert in the United States. When he called Epstein, "I Want to Hold Your Hand" was still well below the Top 40 in the U.S. charts, and he was able to get them for $6,500, plus a share of the ticket sales, for two concerts at Carnegie Hall. By the time Beatlemania was evident, Brian would receive an offer for twice that to have the Beatles perform at Madison Square Garden, which he had to refuse due to scheduling problems.

girlfriends, wives, and families

HOW THEY MET

at The Liverpool College of Art, John met Cynthia Powell, who was in the same year and in the same lettering classes as John. After a few brief conversations John asked Cynthia for a dance in dance class, and then a date. She said she was engaged, which just seemed to make John more determined. "I didn't ask you to marry me, did I?" he replied. They soon were dating frequently.

while in Hamburg, the band was befriended by photographer Astrid Kirchherr, who took many famous pictures of the band in Hamburg. Stuart Sutcliffe and Astrid became engaged two months after they met.

during the Beatles' long stint at the Cavern, Ringo became one of the female fans' favorites. Maureen Cox ran into Ringo one day in 1962 when she was on her way to hairdressing class and got his autograph. On another occasion, she quickly kissed Ringo as he left the Cavern dressing room. Finally, he asked her for a dance at the Cavern and gave her and a friend a ride home afterward.

jane Asher met the Beatles in April 1963, when she interviewed them for *Radio Times*. After she spent the afternoon with the band, Paul drove her home and asked to see her again. Paul said that although all the Beatles were trying to "pull" Jane, he got her with a line from Chaucer: "Ful semyly hir wympul pynched was."

Paul lived with Jane and her parents for nearly three years, and Jane later kept a key to Paul's house in St. John's Wood, London, which he bought in 1966. They fended off questions from reporters about marriage, although Jane seemed to be warmer to the idea than Paul.

An actress since the age of five, when she appeared in the film *Mandy,* Jane continued to pursue her career, which called her away from London frequently. This bothered Paul, but also inspired him to write "I'm Looking Through You" when she left for Bristol to work for the Old Vic Company. She was also the inspiration behind the McCartney compositions "Here, There, and Everywhere" and "And I Love Her."

Jane's mother, Margaret, was a music teacher and gave Paul his first lessons on the recorder. Paul later played recorder for "The Fool on the Hill."

Paul and John used the basement where Jane's mother took her students as a studio, composing "And I Love Her," "Every Little Thing," "Eleanor Rigby," "You Won't See Me," and "I'm Looking Through You," along with many others, on the piano there.

patti Boyd had worked with *A Hard Day's Night* director Dick Lester on his Smith's Crisps commercials, and was cast as one of four schoolgirls who meet the Beatles on a train for their first film. She can be seen in *A Hard Day's Night,* cutting George's hair. George complimented her by comparing her to Brigitte Bardot, but she refused his first request for a date, saying she had a boyfriend, whom she had been seeing for two years. His second request was accepted, however, and she soon moved in with him.

Patti is said to have inspired Harrison's "Something," "For You Blue," and "It's All Too Much."

---

yoko Ono, her husband, and her daughter moved to London in 1966 to take advantage of artistic opportunities offered to Yoko. During her opening at the Indica Gallery on November 9, 1966, she was introduced to John by the gallery's part-owner John Dunbar. She walked up to John, and said nothing, but handed him a card that read "Breathe." John took an interest in her work and sponsored one of her shows in September 1967.

In May 1968, Yoko dropped in to visit John at his home in Weybridge. Her husband was in France with their daughter, and John's wife, Cynthia, was in Greece with friends of the Beatles. After John and Yoko spent the night recording music, which was to become the *Two Virgins* album, Cynthia returned the next day to find Yoko in her house.

---

after her first marriage ended, Linda Eastman began working as a photographer at *Town & Country* magazine. She managed to secure a shoot of the Rolling Stones on a cruise down the Hudson, which led to more work as a photographer to stars such as Stevie Winwood and Warren Beatty. In Austria in 1965, she shot the Beatles during the filming of *Help!*, but did not meet them until their Shea Stadium performance in 1966.

Then, in 1967, she was introduced to Paul by a former member of the Animals at the Bag O' Nails Club on Kingley

Street, London. After their conversation, Linda was invited to the *Sgt. Pepper* party at Brian Epstein's house. When Paul came to New York in May 1969, Linda gave him her phone number and they spent several days together. Paul even baby-sat while Linda went out to shoot at concerts.

coincidentally, Linda and Yoko both attended Sarah Lawrence College in New York state.

linda is the subject of the song "Linda," written by song-writer Jack Lawrence as payment to Linda's father, a copyright lawyer, in 1947. "Linda" was recorded by Jan & Dean in 1963.

BEATLE WEDDINGS

in 1962 Cynthia discovered she was pregnant. John offered to marry her, and the ceremony was carried out, in a very seductive fashion, in Mount Pleasant on August 23, 1962. No parents came, and the rest of the band wore black. By this time, the Beatles were on the verge of fame, and Cynthia saw little of John as he traveled to performances, including one on his wedding night, and recording sessions. Mimi, worried about Cynthia being alone, offered to have her move in.

John and Cynthia's clandestine marriage was reported by the press in fall of 1963, and John finally brought Cynthia and their son Julian to London to live with him, first in a flat in Knightsbridge. They took up residence in a six-bedroom house, "Kenwood," in Surrey in July 1964.

it was during the second trip to Germany that the band lost Stuart Sutcliffe. He decided to marry Astrid Kirchherr and later to reenter art school in Hamburg. He said he thought it would be best for Paul to take over bass guitar, as he was obviously a much more talented musician. Stu started getting headaches and collapsed in school in late 1961. When it happened again in February 1962, he stayed in bed, writing long letters to John. Visits to doctors were no help, and he died of a brain hemorrhage in April 1962.

Stuart Sutcliffe was commemorated by the Beatles in a photograph on the *Sgt. Pepper* album.

similarly, Ringo and Maureen carried on a long-distance relationship while Ringo was in London in late 1964, dating model Vicki Hodge. When Ringo went into the hospital to have his tonsils removed, Maureen rushed down to visit him at the hospital and stayed with him through January, when she became pregnant. Ringo proposed to her on his knees after a night of drinking, and they were married on February 11, 1965.

Brian Epstein was best man, and all the Beatles were in attendance except Paul, who was on vacation. Ringo's and Maureen's parents were in attendance as well.

george and Patti were married, after a one-month engagement—he proposed on Christmas Day—at the Epsom Register Office in Surrey on January 21, 1966. Paul served as witness. They honeymooned in Barbados.

john and Yoko were married on March 20, 1969, in Gibraltar, a quick ceremony arranged while they were on vacation in Paris. Yoko wore a white wide-brimmed hat, a short minidress, and sunglasses. John wore a white jacket and tennis shoes. From there they flew back to Paris to make the announcement. Yoko said, "We are going to stage many happenings and events together. This marriage was one of them." They had an unconventional honeymoon in Amsterdam, where they held their "Bed-In for Peace."

paul had been separated from Jane Asher for five months when he called Linda in November 1969 with an invitation to visit him in London. After living together for a few months, they announced their engagement on March 11, 1969, one day before the wedding. They had booked the wedding at the Marylebone Register Office only the day before. Paul had forgotten to buy a ring, but persuaded a shopkeeper to open his store after hours so he could purchase a gold ring for twelve pounds.

Linda was four months pregnant at the time of the wedding.

BEATLE KIDS

on April 8, 1963, Cynthia gave birth to Julian Lennon at 7:45 A.M. at Sefton General Hospital.

sean Lennon was born to Yoko and John on October 9, 1975 (John's thirty-fifth birthday), at New York Hospital.

ringo and Maureen's first son, Zak, was born on September 13, 1965; their second, Jason, on August 19, 1967; and their daughter, Lee, was born on November 17, 1970.

paul adopted Linda's daughter, Heather, after they were married. Paul and Linda have had three children: Mary, born August 29, 1969; Stella, born September 3, 1971; and James, born September 12, 1977.

patti and George had no children.

DIVORCES AND BREAKUPS

when Cynthia Lennon returned from a vacation in Greece and found Yoko Ono in their house, she sought comfort in a night of drinking with a friend of the Lennons, Alexis Mardas, but ended up sleeping with him. The divorce was finalized on November 8, 1969.

ringo and Maureen's marriage came under severe strain when George Harrison, in the company of his wife, Ringo, and Maureen, declared that he held a passionate love for Ringo's wife. Rumors of various affairs sprang up, and Ringo finally admitted adultery with actress Nancy Andrews. Ringo and Maureen were divorced on July 17, 1975. Ringo attempted to make life easy for Maureen, with a £500,000 settlement and a £250,000 house in London.

on Christmas Day, 1967, Paul proposed to Jane Asher, who was then in America with the Old Vic Company. The engagement was announced in January 1968. However, Jane discovered Paul's affair with an American woman when she dropped by Paul's house unexpectedly, and announced that the engagement was off on July 20, 1968, on a BBC radio program.

late in 1973, Patti and George's marriage began to strain, and Patti realized that she was in love with Eric Clapton, who regularly visited the couple at their home. She traveled with Eric on his American tour, and, although she and George attempted to reconcile, they were divorced in 1977. Patti married Eric Clapton on March 27, 1979. All the former Beatles except John were at the wedding.

the beatles business

lennon admitted to a reporter in 1963 that his professional ambition was "to be rich and famous." At this stage, although the Beatles were working overtime, they had not quite seen the monetary fruits of their labors, which has driven some to speculate that this was the reason for their inclusion of their famous version of "Money (That's What I Want)" on their second album.

other songs about money and management problems include "Taxman," of which George wrote: " 'Taxman' was when I first realized that even though we had started earning money, we were actually giving most of it away in taxes; it was and still is typical. Why should this be so?"

paul and John would joke about the money they made from composing by prefacing a songwriting session with the inspiring statement "Let's write a swimming pool!"

on the Far East and Australia tour, John and Aunt Mimi appeared on a TV interview, and Mimi made a comment about how poor John was at arithmetic. The interviewer then turned to John and asked, "If you're bad at math, how do you count all the money you're earning?" John replied, "I don't count it. I weigh it."

the Beatles became millionaires in 1965.

with the release of three new songs, and the *Anthology* documentary generating interest in the band, the Beatles made their first appearance on *Forbes*'s annual list of the forty highest-paid entertainers in 1995. With estimated earnings for 1994 and 1995 at $130 million, the Beatles came in third, behind Oprah Winfrey (at second with $146 million) and Stephen Spielberg (at $285 million). The Rolling Stones showed up on the list just behind the Beatles, with estimated earnings of $121 million.

BRIAN EPSTEIN

on December 3, 1961, the Beatles met Brian Epstein at his store to discuss the possibility of his managing the band. They met again on December 10, and all agreed that Brian should be manager. A contract was arranged that would take effect from February 1, 1962 and last for five years, with either side having the option to back out with three months' notice. The contract was signed by the Beatles on January 24, 1962. Epstein never signed this contract, asking the Beatles to take him at his word. He said he never cheated them.

Epstein had no previous experience managing bands.

according to one account, Epstein got a ten percent commission on any earnings under £1,500, and fifteen percent on any earnings over £1,500. By 1963 Epstein's percentage rose to twenty-five percent, and his percentage was taken before expenses were deducted.

on June 26, 1962, Brian founded NEMS Enterprises Limited as an entertainment agency separate from the record store. He started with one hundred pounds of shares, divided between himself and his brother. On April 27, 1964, he increased the capital to ten thousand pounds of shares, with five thousand for himself, four thousand for his brother, and two hundred and fifty for each of the Beatles. By March 1964 the company had a staff of fifteen, and by 1966 there were eighty staff members and five offices. During Epstein's life, he signed acts such as Gerry & the Pacemakers, Cilla Black, and Billy J. Kramer.

the Beatles' ten percent share in NEMS was a gift that Epstein was very public about, and exhibited as proof that he was not out to con the band.

in 1963, groups discovered by Epstein took 85 Top Ten songs in the British charts.

the Beatles' manager may have helped in more than the usual ways. Although he denied the story, his associates insisted that he ordered ten thousand copies of the Beatles' first single, "Love Me Do," for his record store in order to place the single on the charts.

after all the dust from the first American tour had settled, Epstein was offered $10,000,000 (over 50 million in 1997 dollars) by a New York investment group for his management contract. He declined.

some have characterized Epstein as a devoted but naive manager. On one occasion, he lost £750,000 to a swindling tax advisor who simply asked him for the money to set up a tax shelter. Another example was his merchandising deal, which took only ten percent of the gross sales. He later renegotiated the merchandising contract in 1964, but only after taking a loss that has been estimated at an incredible 100 million dollars.

when Brian Epstein went into negotiation with United Artists representatives Walter Shenson and Bud Ornstein, they were prepared to offer twenty-five percent of the net, but Epstein, probably still thinking in terms of the Beatles' minuscule royalty from EMI, announced that he would accept no less than seven and a half percent. In the end, lawyer David Jacobs was able to secure twenty-five percent of the net for the band on a three-movie deal.

epstein also failed to take advantage of the expiration of the Beatles' original stingy contract with EMI for a full seventeen months, allowing a ridiculously small royalty to remain intact until the contract was renegotiated in November 1966.

in 1967 the *Financial Times* estimated that Epstein was worth seven million pounds (over 55 million 1997 dollars). When he died later that year, it was discovered that this was a great overestimation due to gambling and lavish spending.

in 1964, Brian signed a deal with Souvenir Press for his autobiography, and passed the ghostwriting on to NEMS employee Derek Taylor, who wrote *A Cellarful of Noise* from a weekend's worth of taped interviews.

brian Epstein was found dead in his bedroom on Saturday, August 26, 1967. He was thirty-two. On September 8, the coroner released a verdict of accidental death due to an overdose of Carbitol, which contains the toxin bromide. He had been taking the pills for insomnia. The coroner decided the death was due to a build-up of bromide in his system, inconsistent with suicides, who take a single large dose. The police found seventeen bottles of pills of various sorts in his house.

memorial services for Brian were held in St. John's Wood, near Paul's house and Abbey Road Studios, on October 17, 1967, and he was buried in the Jewish Cemetery on Long Lane, Aintree, Liverpool. The funeral was a private family gathering—the Beatles did not attend. They did attend the memorial service five weeks later, where the attending rabbi read from the Book of Proverbs: "Sayest thou that the man diligent in his business, he shall stand before kings."

EMI, PARLOPHONE, AND CAPITOL

george Martin admitted that he had nothing to lose by signing the Beatles. They received no advance, and only a penny royalty per single sold for domestic sales, half a penny for foreign sales. An album of twelve songs would count as six singles, and royalties would only increase by one-fourth of a penny after one year and by half a penny after two years. It was not until 1966 that the contract was renegotiated, and the Beatles emerged with an unprecedented royalty of ten percent on the wholesale price of their records, rising to fifteen percent after sales of one hundred thousand copies for singles and thirty thousand copies on albums. In the United States, the royalty schedule rose as high as seventeen and a half percent.

after the initial success of the Beatles, Brian Epstein found George Martin a willing customer for his acts. George signed Cilla Black, Gerry & The Pacemakers, and Billy J. Kramer, all managed by Epstein. In 1963, Epstein and Martin's bands dominated the pop charts, holding the number one spot for a total of thirty-seven weeks. On June 14, 1963, Martin became the very first A&R man behind the three bands holding the top three chart positions, with Billy J. Kramer, Gerry & the Pacemakers, and the Beatles.

while EMI made an out-and-out profit of £2,200,000 (over $30 million in today's dollars) from Martin's acts in 1963, Martin himself was making £3,000 per year (over $40,000 U.S. 1997 dollars), and was denied any Christmas bonus. He attempted to negotiate with EMI, but eventually left to form an independent production firm, and continued to produce his acts for a percentage commission.

the Beatles, especially Paul, had no problem with throwing their weight around EMI when they were displeased. When the proofs for the *Sgt. Pepper* album were delayed, Paul rang around through EMI until he found the one responsible, and let him have it. The proofs were hand delivered immediately with apologies. He later called the EMI chairman, Sir Joseph Lockwood, directly during some difficult negotiations. Lockwood drove over to discuss the matter with Paul face to face.

capitol Records was a wholly owned subsidiary of EMI, but was given independence on its acquisitions, which allowed them to turn the Beatles down repeatedly. When they finally broke in the States beyond anyone's expectations, Brian was able to convince Capitol to put $40,000 (around $200,000 1997 dollars) into advertising and publicity for the band, including a million copies of a four-page newsletter on the band, free copies of Beatles singles for every major DJ in America, five million posters reading "The Beatles are Coming," and photographs of Capitol executives wearing Beatles wigs.

Prior to the Beatles, the most Capitol had spent on an advertising campaign was $5,000.

APPLE CORPS

in 1967 the Beatles were advised that they stood to lose two million pounds to taxes if they didn't invest in a business venture. Apple Corps Ltd. was thus started as a creative outlet for the Beatles and their friends. Paul and John exuded enthusiasm about the experiment in corporate culture, where creative people could play with large sums of money in an unstructured manner. According to John: "It's more of a trick to see if we can get artistic freedom within a business structure." Paul called the experiment "a controlled weirdness . . . a kind of Western communism." Various divisions of the experiment faded one by one, as staff began to use expense accounts for cars and caviar, and large sums disappeared overnight. The venture eventually came to be managed by Eastman & Eastman, Linda Eastman's relatives, and more directly, by Allen Klein, an experienced music manager.

the first musician signed by Apple Records, which turned out to be the only unqualified success under the Apple banner, was James Taylor. The Iveys (who later became known as Badfinger), Jackie Lomax, and Grapefruit would soon follow. Apple Records' distinctive logo, with one side showing a green apple, the other showing the apple in cross-section, took six months to finalize and the efforts of a team of photographers and typographers. Gene Mahon was head designer, and the "copyright reserved" message was provided by the well-known illustrator Alan Aldridge.

apple Records' first release was "Hey Jude," and the second, which displaced "Hey Jude" from number one in the United Kingdom, and nearly did the same in the United States, was "Those Were the Days" recorded by Mary Hopkin and produced by Paul.

some artists on the Apple label complained about a lack of publicity and problems with distribution. James Taylor only rose to fame after leaving the label. There were, however, a number of artists who made an impact on the charts, such as Mary Hopkin and Badfinger. The label stayed afloat until 1976, releasing both McCartney solo albums and Plastic Ono Band albums.

ringo brought an unusual choice to the label in the form of classical composer John Taverner, whose *The Whale* and *Celtic Requiem* were not a great commercial success, but did give Taverner his first recording contract, airplay, and critical acclaim. Ringo's independent label, Ring O' Records, later picked up *The Whale*.

neil Aspinall was appointed managing director of Apple Corps, and found a home for the venture at number 3 Savile Row, a five-story building dating back to the 1730s in London's West End, which the company reportedly purchased for £500,000.

in 1967 Apple Corps opened a boutique on Baker Street in London and paid the Dutch design group the Fool £100,000 to design the storefront and displays. Seven months later, it was found that the store had lost nearly £200,000 (over 2.5 million in 1997 dollars!), sometimes to shoplifting, sometimes to the staff, and the store was closed. However, instead of auctioning off the remaining £10,000 worth of stock, the stock was quietly given away to anyone who walked into the store. Once the word got out, however, there was a proper Beatles-type riot, and twelve policemen were called in to control the shoppers. Both Paul and John said that the band was tired of keeping a shop.

alex Mardas, aka "Magic Alex," headed the electronics division, which turned out to be more of a non-profit personal research and development department. He designed a seventy-two-track recording machine for the Beatles, and worked on "wallpaper loudspeakers," "domestic force fields," and "nothing boxes." He failed to bring a single product to market during his time at Apple.

the recording machine was part of Alex's project to build for the Beatles a state-of-the-art studio in the basement of 3 Savile Row. The band attempted to record there during the "Get Back" sessions, but found that even the basic needs of a recording studio—sound insulation from the air conditioning unit, for example—were lacking. The grand seventy-two-track console was sold to an electronics shop for five pounds. The sessions were continued with equipment from Abbey Road.

another key ingredient to the Apple empire was Caleb (no known surname), a psychic who authorized business dealings through Tarot, the *I Ching,* or astrology. He eventually left out of boredom.

after six months, Apple Corps had spent 1.4 million pounds ($18 million in 1997 dollars), and all four Beatles were overdrawn on their corporate partnership account, with Paul being the greatest spender, and John a close second. They were advised to bring in professional help, curb spending, and fire those who were taking advantage.

in January 1969, John Lennon told a *Rolling Stone* reporter that if Apple kept spending money at its current rate, it would be broke in six months. Paul was upset about this information getting out, but John continued to confirm that it was the case, causing yet another point of contention for the band.

BEATLES STUFF FOR SALE

when Beatlemania broke, a factory in a London suburb started producing Beatle wigs, and claimed they took orders from Buckingham Palace and Eton.

reporter: "How do you feel about teenagers imitating you with Beatle wigs?"

john: "They're not imitating us, because we don't wear Beatle wigs."

beatle-related products brought in an estimated $50 million (over $250 million in 1997 dollars) in the U.S. in 1964.

sotheby's first auction of former Beatle possessions was held in June 1979, and proved such a success that the auction house started an annual rock 'n' roll memorabilia auction in 1981 in London. The first item to be sold was John's old Steinway piano, which was valued at £1,000 and went for

£7,500. Paul's, although in worse condition, went for £9,000. A letter from George to Stuart Sutcliffe in Hamburg, asking him to return to Liverpool, received a winning bid of £500 in 1984.

in 1984, Yoko Ono placed 117 of John's old possessions on sale at Sotheby's in New York.

among the other items sold through auctions are John's costume for the role of the ugly sister in a 1959 Liverpool College of Art production of *Cinderella*, an early draft of the *Yellow Submarine* script, an early sketch of the "running Indian monster" for *Yellow Submarine*, two tapes of a 1969 interview with John and Yoko by Australian DJ Tony MacArthur that was never aired, and a 1956 school photo of Liverpool Institute High School, which shows Paul with his classmates.

after the group stayed in Kansas City during their first American tour, two merchandisers bought the pillowcases used by the Beatles at their hotel for $1,000. The cases were cut into 160,000 one-inch squares, and sold to fans within a week for a dollar each, making a clear profit of over $800,000 in 1997 U.S. dollars.

the "official" merchandising company in the United States in the 1960s was Seltaeb ("Beatles" spelled backwards), who used the Beatles' likenesses to sell masks, buttons, and ice cream, among at least 150 other items. Their original contract, which gave NEMS only a ten percent share, was renegotiated in August 1964, and NEMS' share rose to forty-six percent.

a sheet of paper with lyrics to "Dear Prudence" in John's writing, along with several lines of verse and doodles around the edges, was sold at a 1987 Sotheby's auction for $19,500.

lennon's manuscript for one song on the *A Hard Day's Night* album, "If I Fell," was auctioned at Sotheby's in London in April 1988 and fetched £7,800, while the manuscript of "Any Time at All," the eighth song on the album, went for £9,000.

a world record for the sale of a Beatles manuscript was set in September 1995 at Sotheby's in London. Lyrics to "Getting Better" written in Paul's writing were sold in auction for close to $250,000.

BEATLES SONGS FOR SALE

northern Songs was established as the publisher for Lennon/McCartney compositions in 1963 by Dick James, who administered the company through Dick James Music Ltd. In the beginning, fifty percent of Northern Songs was owned by James and his partner, twenty percent by John, another twenty by Paul, and ten percent by Brian Epstein. In 1965 a portion of the company was floated on the London Stock Exchange, and three thousand investors bought in, leaving John and Paul with fifteen percent ownership each, NEMS with seven and a half percent, and George and Ringo with small shares as well. Dick James and his partner kept twenty-three percent. By 1967, the share price had quintupled.

Dick James became resented by Paul and John, who, although they had agreed to the deal, realized that they didn't own their creative endeavors. In December 1964, Dick James returned to his vocalist roots with the album *Sing a Song of Beatles,* a Christmas album backed up by a 100-member chorus. While they were working on *Magical Mystery Tour,* James tried to get them to write songs for Barbra Streisand, who was interested in covering some Beatles songs. John's reply was a curt "Fuck off."

In 1969, Dick James quietly sold his share of the company to ATV, the media giant chaired by Sir Lew Grade, who had been asking for the sale for years. James made over a million pounds for his percentage, and ATV quickly moved in on the rest of the shares with an offer of nine and a half million pounds ($99 million in 1997 dollars).

John and Paul were both out of the country when James made his sale, and learned of the deals days after the fact. By the time Allen Klein, manager of the Stones and other well-known acts, was called in, a third factor in the form of a consortium of investors had come into the picture. Klein and Grade took turns trying to woo the investors to their side. While the investors were at first suspicious of Klein, they worked out a deal whereby he would exclude himself from the company's management, and after several months of very tense negotiations, it appeared as though Apple might gain control of the Lennon/McCartney compositions. These hopes were dashed when John angrily reacted to what he perceived as an attempt by the investors to control his music. "I'm sick of being fucked about by men in suits sitting on their fat arses in the City," he said. On May 20, ATV became the effective controllers of Northern Songs.

the publishing rights to the Beatles' first two recordings, "Love Me Do" and "How Do You Do It," were given to a subsidiary of EMI, and Paul was able eventually to regain control of these rights.

a number of songs have been picked up, despite high price tags, for advertisements. "We Can Work It Out" was used by Hewlett-Packard for advertisements in the U.K.

rights to the song *Help!* were purchased by the Ford Motor Company in the 1980s for a reported $100,000, but the song was rerecorded for their Lincoln–Mercury ads.

in 1987 Nike bought rights to use "Revolution" in an advertising blitz for a reported $250,000, provoking the ire of the surviving Beatles and many of their fans. Yoko Ono joined the Beatles in a suit against Nike, EMI, and Capitol. This happened while Paul was still in a campaign to regain control over the Beatles' songs.

a version of "Something" appeared in a commercial for the Chrysler LeBaron Coupe in the late 1980s.

"with a Little Help from My Friends" turned up as the theme song to the TV program about growing up in the sixties, *The Wonder Years.*

alf Bicknell, chauffeur to the Beatles for four years, at home and on tour, received four tapes from John in the 1960s. One was of John attempting to complete a demo of "If I Fell," another has George working on his first composition, and a third is a voice tape of the Beatles doing comic readings of the Bible. Bicknell expected £60,000 for the tapes when he put them on auction in 1989, but only made £12,000 for two of them. The same year, Bicknell published his memoirs, *Baby You Can Drive My Car,* coauthored by Garry Marsh and with an introduction by George Harrison.

MANAGEMENT PROBLEMS

when the problems with the Beatles' Apple Corps—including not only mismanagement, but outright theft—became evident, a rift in the band occurred over who would take over management of the band and the corporation. John and Yoko favored Allen Klein, and were supported by George and Ringo, while Paul favored the law firm of Eastman & Eastman, headed by Lee Eastman, father of his new wife, Linda.

klein was a well-known manager and representative of acts such as the Shirelles, Bobby Vinton, and Sam Cooke. Under his management, Cooke became the first pop star to receive a million-dollar advance on royalties. In 1965 Klein became business advisor for the Rolling Stones, and before long was their sole manager. The Stones were happy with his management, and Mick Jagger informed the Beatles that, although the Stones were selling fewer records than the Beatles, they were making much more money, due to Klein's negotiations. Klein repeatedly approached the Beatles, until he finally got John, Ringo, and George to agree to have him take over Apple Corps. Paul walked out of that particular meeting.

paul had already brought in John Eastman, Linda's brother, as advisor and contract manager. Eastman was involved in an attempt to buy NEMS on behalf of the Beatles, an attempt thwarted, according to Eastman, by Klein, who was outspokenly critical of NEMS and the money he said they owed the band. When the deal fell through, it became apparent that the Eastmans and Klein could never work together. All the Beatles but Paul signed Klein as business manager on May 20, 1969, while Paul retained Eastman. Paul subsequently regularly refused to attend meetings with Klein, sending instead his lawyer, Charles Corman.

klein's first move was to attempt to renegotiate the Beatles' royalty agreement with both their British and American companies. He brought all four members of the band into a meeting with Sir Joseph Lockwood, chairman of EMI, and announced his intention. Lockwood replied, "All right, we can talk about it. Provided both sides get some benefit, there's no harm in renegotiating." Klein replied, "No, you don't understand. *You* don't get anything. *We* get more." Lockwood ordered them out. Klein reportedly called back in a half hour with apologies.

klein, however, did get a royalty of twenty-five percent of retail price on U.S. records from Capitol, which was then supposed to be the highest royalty yet paid out to a band by a record company.

klein further alienated Paul when he brought in Phil Spector to assemble an album out of the recordings made during the "Get Back" sessions, which would become *Let It Be*. Paul was outraged by Spector's production of "The Long and Winding Road," and Spector was unavailable when Paul tried to complain. Spector's version was released, leaving one more reason for the Beatles to break up.

although Klein's tactics and deals have been criticized, it was later revealed during Paul's lawsuit that Klein, in eighteen months, made more money for the Beatles than Epstein had in the entire course of his management.

according to Paul's authorized biography, when Paul sued the other Beatles to break the partnership, he based his case on Klein's supposed incompetence and less than aboveboard dealings. When Paul's lawyers researched the case, they found only one case of Klein's mismanagement: a check from Capitol which Paul said proved that he overcharged the Beatles by £500,000.

lawsuits and pr gaffes

for Paul's twenty-first birthday, a huge party was thrown at his Aunt Jinny's house, with Liverpool band the Scaffold performing. This wild night also marked John's last fistfight, with a local disk jockey. "I smashed him up," claimed John, "I broke his bloody ribs for him. I was pissed at the time. He'd called me a queer." The disk jockey, Bob Wooler, sued, but reportedly settled for £200 and an apology. The telegram, which included the message "Really sorry Bob terribly worried to realize what I had done Stop what more can I say John Lennon," was sold for 550 pounds at a Sotheby's auction in 1984.

in 1965 John commented to a *Playboy* reporter that Ringo had been with the group for a while before Pete Best was let go, filling in during Pete's allegedly frequent illnesses. Ringo followed up on this comment with, "He took little pills to make him ill." Pete sued over this comment, and reportedly took an out-of-court settlement.

when Capitol Records in the U.S. finally agreed to sign the Beatles, their promotional material and press releases contained wild inaccuracies such as the story of their discovery by Epstein in Hamburg, and spelled Paul's name as "McCatney."

many inaccuracies reported in the press originated with the Beatles themselves. According to Paul, to alleviate the pressure of doing interviews, they would "try and plant lies to the press." Paul recalls that one of the best ones that got printed was that George was Tommy Steele's cousin.

john Lennon made his notorious remark about the Beatles being more popular than Christ in an interview in an informal setting with Maureen Cleave of the *Evening Standard:*

> Christianity will go. It will vanish and shrink. I needn't argue about that; I'm right and will be proved right. We're more popular than Jesus now; I don't know which will go first, rock 'n' roll or Christianity. Jesus was all right, but his disciples were thick and ordinary. It's them twisting it that ruins it for me.

It was several months before the comment was reported in the United States, and when it was, Epstein received reports of burnings of Beatles records in Nashville. When he arrived in New York, he learned that the Ku Klux Klan had been burning the Beatles in effigy, and that a Cleveland minister had threatened Beatles fans in his congregation with excommunication. Newspaper publisher Carl L. Estes later called for the Beatles' deportation and said they should be "fumigated." John made a televised apology: "I'm not anti-God, anti-Christ, or anti-religion. I was not saying we are greater or better." And later in the press conference: "I believe in God, but not as one thing, not as an old man in the sky. I believe that what people call God is something in all of us."

Maureen Cleave herself remarked that John's comments were taken out of context. "He did not mean to boast about the Beatles' fame," she said.

Years later while furthering his spirituality, he reflected, "I suppose I wouldn't make that remark about Jesus today. I think about things differently. I think Buddhism is simple and more logical than Christianity, but I've nothing against Jesus."

"**come** Together," which John penned, resulted in a lawsuit against him, alleging that he stole the two opening lines and the opening melody from Chuck Berry's "You Can't Catch Me." John reportedly settled, but still flatly denied that he plagiarized. The settlement reportedly was that John would record three songs from Berry's publishing company, Big Seven Music.

John says that the song is "gobbledygook," but that he got the title from Timothy Leary, who used the slogan around the time he was running for governor of California against Ronald Reagan.

fans and fanatics

beatlemania erupted suddenly on October 13, 1963, when the Beatles performed at the London Palladium for the TV program *Sunday Night at the London Palladium,* broadcast live to an audience of 15,000,000. At the beginning of the show, the compere, Bruce Forsyth, introduced the act and told viewers they would be back in forty-two minutes. Uncounted fans descended on the venue, blocking the stage door and attempting to get gifts and telegrams through to the band.

quickly, other TV stations sent news crews to cover the phenomenon, and the police found themselves completely unprepared. The Beatles exited through the front door, as the stage door was blocked, and had to make a fifty-yard dash for their waiting car. The next day, the *Daily Mirror* invented the term "Beatlemania" to describe the pandemonium.

The Beatles, however, interpreted Beatlemania as beginning on October 31, 1963, when thousands of fans gathered to welcome them home from their Swedish tour.

one couldn't say they didn't work for their fans' adulation: In 1963, the Beatles released two albums, four EPs, and four singles. They went on seven tours and made over two hundred live performances. 1964 saw the band's first movie, *A Hard Day's Night,* two British albums, five U.S. Albums, four tours, and three U.K. singles. "The reason we were twice as good as anybody else is we worked twice as hard as anybody else" was a comment attributed to both Paul and George.

in Liverpool in 1963, the homes of the band became tourist shops, with some fans traveling all the way from America to spend the night in the yards of the Beatles' parents. The McCartneys would sometimes invite fans in for tea, and Ringo's parents found pieces of their door missing and messages written on their walls.

on the day the Beatles arrived in New York for the first time, radio deejays took to announcing the temperature in "Beatle degrees" and the time in "Beatle minutes."

on their first American tour, the Beatles were forced to make use of ambulances to safely leave the shows. At the Cow Palace in San Francisco, their limousine was covered by fans, who caved in the roof, and the band was taken to a nearby ambulance which was full of intoxicated sailors who had earlier been involved in a row. In Seattle, the limo was sent out as a decoy while the Beatles were rushed off in an ambulance. The empty limo's trunk was crushed and its door handles ripped off.

door handles were also removed from hotels where the Beatles stayed by fans who wanted something, anything that the four might have touched.

the noise made by the crowds at Beatles concerts was measured by experts on at least one occasion. The one who did so in Australia claimed that the fans' noise was louder than a jet plane.

in Seattle, a female fan who was attempting to get backstage fell twenty-five feet down a ventilation shaft and dropped onto the floor at Ringo's feet. He asked her if she was sure she was all right, but she ran from him and disappeared into the crowd.

in Chicago, 15,000 tickets for the Beatles' September 5, 1964, appearance at the International Amphitheater sold out in hours, leaving about 4,000 fans desperate for tickets. Some were so overwhelmed that they threatened suicide if they weren't allowed in.

in Boston, a young hoodlum stole a fan's ticket at knifepoint, but was captured at the concert because the fan had memorized his seat number.

in California, fans were spotted eating grass that Ringo had trod upon. When asked his opinion of this show of devotion, Ringo replied, "I just hope they don't get indigestion."

in 1964, fans wanted Ringo's internal body parts. When word got out that his tonsils were being removed, he was showered with requests (one account says he received over a thousand) for the unused bits. It was soon announced that they would be incinerated.

the Official Beatles Fan Club was started in 1962 by Bobbie Brown of Liverpool. In a little over six months, they had one thousand members, and received over thirty letters a day. It closed in March 1972, after ten years of operation, but a number of unofficial clubs have been launched throughout the world. The club, which was at its peak in 1965 with 80,000 members, always lost money. Members received, besides regular bulletins and newsletters, a special "Sgt. Pepper" photo which cost the club 700 pounds, and special Beatles Christmas records, available only to fan club members. These Christmas records, collected in 1970 as an album, included tracks such as "Rudolph the Red-Nosed Ringo," "Good King Wenceslas," "Please Don't Bring Your Banjo Back," and "Everywhere It's Christmas."

the official Beatle periodical, *Beatles Monthly,* was started in 1963 by Beat Publications, which paid for its official status.

At its best, it achieved a circulation of 80,000 copies in Britain, and appeared as a supplement to *Datebook* magazine in the States.

the Beatles attempted various schemes to get around fans or through situations unnoticed. The band attempted costumes at one stage to get through a customs point without causing a disturbance. George and John were recognized, but Paul kept up the disguise by pretending to be an eccentric photographer talking "psychological gibberish."

after the Beatles stopped touring, Paul had a mustache made professionally, to match the color of his hair, and bought a pair of thick-framed glasses in order to wander around France.

paul claimed that fans around his home in St. John's Wood, London, broke into his house and stole memorabilia, including clothes and a photograph of his father. He says he wrote "She Came In Through the Bathroom Window" after a fan did just that.

paul also recalled a time he saw a fan in the street who was wearing a jacket just like one that had been stolen from his house. After he ripped it off her, she said to him, "It's the wrong size, it's mine." Paul realized his mistake and apologized.

most of the time, Paul had an amicable distant relationship with the core of fans who surrounded his home in St. John's Wood, London. "I gave him three peaches in a bag once," one fan recalled. "He'd eaten one of them by the time he got down the Abbey Road front steps. Another time, we shouted out, 'What do you want for your birthday?' He thought for a minute, then he said, 'I haven't got any slippers.'" Slippers were quickly produced and handed over.

george also suffered break-ins. "They come into the garden and rush around," said Patti Harrison to an interviewer. "They got into our bedroom the other day and stole a pair of my trousers and George's pajamas."

charles Manson's obsession with the Beatles included a belief that they were the four angels of Revelation, and that the "White Album" was a prophecy. He interpreted a message of race war in America from the songs "Blackbird," "Piggies," "Happiness Is a Warm Gun," and "Helter Skelter." Lennon remarked on Manson's lunacy, but also compared him to the more sane fans who looked for hidden meanings: "He's like any other Beatles kind of fan who reads mysticism into it. I mean, we used to have a laugh putting this or the other in, in a light-hearted way."

when the Beatles arrived at Kennedy Airport, New York, for their first U.S. concerts, they were greeted at the airport by 10,000 fans; however, the largest crowd ever to turn out to see the Beatles was not in the United States or in Britain, but at the South Australian capital, Adelaide, in June 1964. The crowd of 300,000 had gathered just to see the Beatles arrive and watch their hotel balcony for another glimpse. The band gave two performances at Centennial Hall, and the line for tickets was 250,000 strong, with fans waiting sixty to seventy hours for the tickets that sold out in a mere five.

in Hong Kong, fans paid seventy-five Hong Kong dollars, equivalent to an average week's wages, to see the Beatles. The band complained about the prices when they heard about them.

in Christchurch, New Zealand, in June 1964, a young female fan broke the police line, flew off the Beatles' car, and ended up in the street. The band picked her up, unharmed, and took her to tea at their hotel.

after Beatlemania cooled a bit, some members made attempts to restore their normal life by sneaking out to bars or cinemas. John and Ringo even ventured onto a London bus. They had never been on a London Transport bus before. They were recognized, but took it in stride, filming the passengers and listening to the female conductor's dirty jokes.

while working on *Magical Mystery Tour,* Paul made it into a pub in Perranporth without being recognized, got a pint of beer, and sat down at the piano. Eventually someone recognized him, and he kept the pub open until 2:00 A.M., running through all of his favorite pub songs. He refused, however, to play any Beatles songs.

the most dedicated of the fans named themselves the Apple Scruffs. Many were from the United States, and distinguished themselves by devoting years to watching the Beatles from outside their homes, Abbey Road, and the Apple Corps headquarters. In 1970 they launched a fanzine, which contained such detail about the precise movements of the Beatles that the staff of Apple Corps began reading it monthly. The Apple Scruffs gave it up in 1973, after the Apple Corps headquarters at 3 Savile Row had closed.

other fans were not so innocuous. One woman from America camped out in the lounge of 3 Savile Row with her husband and four children waiting to see John and Yoko, and spending much of her time naked. She had been instructed by higher powers during an acid trip that she was to take the star and his new beau to Fiji.

in 1970, *Rolling Stone* named John Lennon the man of the year, and proclaimed, "A five-hour talk between John Lennon and Richard Nixon would be more significant than any

Geneva Summit Conference between the U.S.A. and Russia."

"PAUL IS DEAD"

shortly after the release of *Abbey Road,* Detroit disk jockey Russ Gibbs proposed that Paul had, on November 9 or 10, 1966, left the studio in anger and was subsequently decapitated in a car crash. He went on to theorize that Brian Epstein had covered up this fact and replaced Paul with a look-alike. Gibbs backed up his theory with "clues" from the album's packaging, and very suddenly, other "clues" began to be found on other packages and song lyrics.

on *Abbey Road,* Paul appears barefoot on the front cover, supposedly evoking a Mafia or Grecian burial ritual. A reviewer took the album cover to represent the group as a funeral procession, with John (dressed in a white suit) as preacher, Paul as corpse, Ringo as undertaker, and George as gravedigger. Paul also appears out of step with the rest, and holds a cigarette in his right hand (Paul was left-handed). A car appears on the front cover with the license plate 28IF, taken to mean Paul would have been twenty-eight if he had not been killed (he was actually twenty-seven). On the back cover, the crack through the street sign is taken as a symbol of the Beatles' disunity, and skulls and religious symbols have been spotted in the shadows.

in 1986, the Volkswagen with the 28IF license plate sold at a Sotheby's auction for £2,300.

the American alternative magazine *Rat Subterranean News* ran a story by Lee Merrick which claimed to have discovered Paul's impostor—Billy Shears, the character the Beatles mentioned on the *Sgt. Pepper* title track. Merrick claimed that he discovered that Shears was a London musician who looked just like Paul, and that Brian Epstein had convinced the Beatles to keep Paul's death a secret and let Shears step in after a little plastic surgery. Merrick even claimed to have substantiated the story through a conversation with Shears's father. The article was published on October 29, 1969.

believers in this strange myth can hear John saying "I buried Paul" in "Strawberry Fields Forever." In fact he is saying, without any sensible reason, "Cranberry sauce."

on the cover of *Sgt. Pepper's Lonely Hearts Club Band,* the hand above Paul's head has been taken as a symbol of death. The flowers which spell out "Beatles" were supposed to be Paul's grave, and some see "PAUL?" in the flowers in the shape of a guitar. The back cover shows George pointing to the first lyric of "She's Leaving Home," which refers to 5 o'clock on a Wednesday morning, and is taken to be the time and day of Paul's death in a car wreck. Paul's back is turned on the back cover. On the front cover, the "actor who took Paul's place" is wearing a black arm band with the letters "O.P.D."—"Ontario Police Department" or "Officially Pronounced Dead"?

the line referring to an unidentified man blowing his mind out in a car is supposed to refer to Paul's fatal accident. John has said that it actually refers to the death of Guinness heir Tara Browne, who drove his sportscar into a parked van at 110 miles per hour in a wealthy London neighborhood in December 1966. The twenty-one-year-old was a friend of the Beatles and other rock musicians. Another car crash reference appears in Ringo's "Don't Pass Me By."

the album package for *Magical Mystery Tour* shows a black walrus, which the cult of Paul-is-dead take as a Scandinavian death symbol. On "Glass Onion," recorded a year later, John sings "The walrus was Paul." The booklet released with the album shows Paul again with a hand above his head, as in the package for *Sgt. Pepper*. In one part of the film, which appeared as a still in the booklet, the Beatles appear with red carnations pinned to their jackets, while Paul wears a black carnation. He claims they ran out of white carnations. In another photo, Paul appears with a sign that reads "I WaS."

on "I Am the Walrus," members of a Shakespearean acting group quote death-related lines.

playing "I'm So Tired" backward is supposed to reveal John chanting, "Paul is dead, man, miss him, miss him."

in 1969, Dr. Henry M. Truby, Director of the University of Miami's Language and Linguistics Research Laboratory, used a spectrograph to test Paul's vocals on later Beatle recordings, and concluded that there was a "reasonable doubt" that Paul's voice belonged to the same person on all the recordings. All the other Beatles' voices were consistent, but Dr. Truby stated, "I hear three different McCartneys."

FANS AND BEATLE WIVES

cynthia Lennon was spared much of the hatred of Beatles fans that Yoko Ono and Linda McCartney would experience. On one occasion, fans surrounding a Miami hotel identified her for a security guard who wouldn't let her into the Beatles' suite. A Cynthia Lennon Fan Club even sprung up in London. However, she did get the occasional obscene phone call or threat from a fan in London, and was even spat at outside the gates of their Cromwell Road home. This became part of their decision to move to the country.

maureen and Ringo kept their dates quiet while in Liverpool, as the female Beatles fans from the Cavern were prone to violent jealousy. One day a fan recognized Ringo's car as Maureen was waiting for Ringo in it. The young fan approached and asked if they were going out. Maureen said no, but the woman reached through the open window, scratching and beating her. "I got the window up just in time," Maureen told Beatles biographer Hunter Davies. "If I hadn't, she would have opened the door and killed me."

news of Paul and Linda's wedding provoked a harsh reaction from the core of fans who surrounded Paul's house. According to one fan, Paul tried to talk to them the day before at the gates, saying, "Look, girls, be fair. I had to get married sometime." After the ceremony, his gates were torn open and burning papers were shoved through his mailbox. The police broke up the crowd. One fan claimed that he wanted to talk to the group again, but they were gone. "He couldn't believe we'd all gone away. . . . When he came back into the house he was almost in tears," said one fan.

yoko Ono received perhaps the worst insults from fans, who called her "yellow" and "chink" outside Abbey Road and John's home.

critics, politicians, and the older generation

shortly after the onset of Beatlemania, the band received their first Royal recognition in the form of an invitation to appear at the Royal Variety Performance with Marlene Dietrich and Maurice Chevalier. Their performance was later broadcast on the BBC.

For the last number, John asked for audience participation: "Will the people in the cheaper seats clap your hands? And the rest of you, if you'll just rattle your jewelry." The slightly subversive remark was welcomed with laughter.

they also received official recognition of a different sort: questions in Parliament over why thousands of policemen were being required to risk their safety for the safety of the Beatles. One minister suggested that the police simply pull out and watch the results. Instead, on November 14, 1963, they turned firehoses on the fans at Plymouth.

the conservative *Daily Telegraph* was equally bitter about the phenomenon, comparing the Beatles to Hitler in their ability to incite mass hysteria. The *Daily Mirror* responded with: "You have to be a real sour square not to love the nutty, noisy, happy, handsome Beatles." The *Daily Mirror* became the first paper after the mania broke to get a long interview with the Beatles, on September 10, 1963, with Donald Zec.

the *Times* music critic William Mann was the first mainstream voice to seriously analyze the Beatles' music. His December 27, 1963, article named John and Paul "the outstanding English composers of 1963." He further compared one of their songs, "Not a Second Time," to Mahler's "Song of the Earth" and remarked on the Beatles' use of the "Aeolian cadence." The *Sunday Times* was next, calling the songwriters "the greatest composers since Beethoven."

the British Communist Party publication *Daily Worker* got in on the game with social commentary, saying that they could hear in the Beatles' music "the voice of 80,000 crumbling houses and 30,000 people on the dole" in Liverpool.

at the end of 1963, in a poll by the *New Musical Express* the Beatles received 14,666 votes for world's best group, and 18,623 in the "British Vocal Section." The year before, they had received 3,906 votes.

in 1964, Ringo was voted vice-president of Leeds University, beating a former Lord Chief Justice in the election.

the Beatles' arrival in Washington coincided with that of British Prime Minster Sir Alec Douglas-Home, who decided to push back his Washington visit by a day. This gave President Lyndon Johnson the opening to say to Douglas-Home, "I liked your advance party, but don't you feel they need haircuts?"

after the Beatles' first *Ed Sullivan Show* appearance, reactions by the press were not all positive. *Newsweek* printed: "Visually they are a nightmare: tight, dandified Edwardian beatnik suits and great pudding bowls of hair. Musically they are a near disaster, guitars and drums slamming out a merciless beat that does away with secondary rhythms, harmony and melody." Billy Graham tuned in, even though the broadcast was on Sunday, and proclaimed them "a passing phase." "A plague has swept the land, but we have been left whole," wrote another commentator, who thought the mania would subside as soon as the Beatles left the States.

elvis was among those who felt that the moptops were less than a good influence on America's youth. He even went as far with this opinion as to raise the issue with the FBI during a visit. An agent reported in an internal memo: "Presley indicated that he is of the opinion that the Beatles laid the groundwork for many of the problems we are having with young people by their filthy, unkempt appearance and suggestive music."

another was William F. Buckley, Jr., who said Beatlemania was a genetic phenomenon: "I tell you, my friends, it is a sickness, which is not a cultivated hallucinatory weakness, but something that derives from a lamentable and organic imbalance. If our children can listen avariciously to the Beatles, it must be because through our genes we have transmitted to them some disorder of the kind. What was our sin? Was it our devotion to Frank Sinatra? How could that be? We who worshipped at the shrine of purity. . . . We may not know what it was, even as Oedipus did not know, during all those years, the reasons why he was cursed."

on June 11, 1965, the Beatles were offered the honor of being made Members of the Order of the British Empire (MBE). Although presented by the Queen, it is the lowest grade of award for civilians. Prime Minister Harold Wilson had suggested the Beatles for the award. Dozens of former recipients returned their awards and filed protest for the "debasement" of their award, while others, such as Lord Netherthrope, voiced their approval. The award was presented on October 26, 1965. One hundred eighty-two others were at Buckingham Palace to receive awards. When the Queen asked Paul how long the band had been together, Ringo replied, "Forty years." In a press conference afterward, Paul replied to the question of what he would do with the medal with: "What you normally do with medals. Put them in a box."

george told a reporter that when they first received notification of the award by mail, they thought that the official envelope and 10 Downing Street return address meant they were being drafted.

john was never comfortable with the medal, and gave it to Mimi, who displayed it proudly. He later lied in an interview about having smoked pot in Her Majesty's bathroom, and eventually sent his chauffeur to collect the award from Mimi, which he wrapped in paper with this message to the Queen: "I am returning this MBE in protest against Britain's involvement in the Nigeria–Biafra thing, against our support of America in Vietnam and against 'Cold Turkey' slipping down the charts. With Love. John Lennon." "Cold Turkey" was a song by John's Plastic Ono Band.

in 1968, the Queen held a meeting of the Council of Knights Bachelor, and in attendance was Sir Joseph Lockwood, Chairman of EMI. The Queen greeted Sir Lockwood with the question, "The Beatles are turning awfully *funny,* aren't they?"

beatle style

klaus Voorman, Astrid Kirchherr, and Jürgen Vollmer, the Beatles' friends in Hamburg, all played a part developing the Beatles' style. Although the Beatles were going all-out for a rough rocker look, they took notice of the collarless suit jackets and combed-forward "French style" haircuts worn by Klaus, Astrid, and their friends. Stu was the first to have his hair cut, by Astrid, and Jürgen cut John's and Paul's hair in this fashion when they visited him in Paris.

the Beatles were constantly asked about the inspiration for their haircuts by reporters, and answered in a variety of ways.

reporter: "Where did you get your hairstyle?"

paul: "From Napoleon. And Julius Caesar too."

Or:

reporter: "Tell me about your hair-dos."

john: "You mean hair-don'ts."

george: "We were coming out of a swimming bath in Liverpool, and we liked the way it looked.

john told Ringo immediately after he was hired that he would have to shave his beard, but he could keep his sideburns.

after cleaning up their appearance as advised by Epstein, John felt strange returning to Liverpool after their national tours: "We felt embarrassed in our suits and being very clean. We were worried that friends might think we'd sold out. Which we had, in a way."

john's "little rebellion" against the cleaned-up appearance of the Beatles was to let his tie hang crooked with the top button of his shirt open.

during interviews and press conferences, the Beatles popularized Liverpudlian phrases such as "fab," "wack," and "gear." The term "grotty" was spuriously introduced through Alun Owen's screenplay for *A Hard Day's Night*. Although he insisted that it came from Liverpool slang for gross, nasty, or unappealing, none of the Beatles had ever heard or used the term. However, the word became and still is in common usage in Britain.

george outlined in an interview one of the major reasons behind the Beatles' fame: "We never lost our sense of humor. I think that's why people liked us, not just because of our music, but because we said funny and outrageous things and were real people."

the footwear that eventually became known as "Beatle boots" was made by Anello and Davide of London. In 1961, Paul and John noticed a pair of flamenco-style boots in their shop window and each bought a pair. George and Pete followed suit when they saw the band leaders wearing them in Liverpool. The shoemakers were commissioned to make footwear for the band's 1964 U.S. tour.

the Beatles bought their suits from Dougie Millings, who drew on a steward's uniform as inspiration for the collarless jackets, and provided them with the gray wool and mohair suits worn on the first American tour. Millings, who turned up as the tailor in *A Hard Day's Night,* was also outfitter to Cliff Richard, Tommy Steele, and Billy Fury. Another of his designs appears on the waxwork figures of the Beatles on the *Sgt. Pepper* cover.

relocating out of London, John bought a home in a development in Weybridge, Surrey, where Ringo also lived. John bought the house for £20,000 (over a quarter of a million in 1997 U.S. dollars), but spent twice that on decoration and landscaping. He had his £11,000 Rolls-Royce painted in extravagant psychedelic colors, with a zodiac sign on the top, and had a large caravan outside his house painted to match.

He kept five cats in the house, where he lived with Cynthia until Yoko came along.

upstairs, John had two rooms set up to accommodate his car racing collection. John owned twenty sets of model cars and a variety of tracks. He brought one of his favorite sets with him on the Beatles' first U.S. tour and had it set up backstage.

paul took a place in St. John's Wood, London, very close to the Abbey Road Studios. The house cost him forty thousand pounds, and he spent twenty thousand on redecorations. In contrast to John, he did little in the way of landscaping, and let the garden grow wild. He bought a Mini Cooper with tinted windows and an Aston-Martin. He regularly took his English sheepdog, Martha, for walks in nearby Primrose Hill or Regent's Park.

after moving in, Paul began buying Magrittes. Magritte's *Le Jeu de Mourre* was the inspiration for the Apple Records logo. He also bought a commissioned piece by Peter Blake and a sculpture by Eduardo Paolozzi, who was Stu Sutcliffe's teacher in Hamburg.

paul also bought his father a five-bedroom mock-Tudor home outside Liverpool, in Heswall, with views of the River Dee. He spent £8,750 and another £8,000 on decoration and improvements. Paul would use the house, known as Rembrandt, as a retreat for songwriting.

george opted for a single-story house in Esher on a private development. He included no Beatles memorabilia, gold records, or awards in his decor, choosing instead simple pinewood furniture and souvenirs from his travels in India. He kept no chairs, using merely cushions on the floor. The two wings of the bungalow wrap around a courtyard in back with a heated swimming pool.

ringo's house was more expensive than John's, thirty-seven thousand pounds, even though it was part of the same development. He also took forty thousand to landscape and renovate, mostly concentrating on the garden. He had a large amphitheater dug and terraced with brick and ponds. Inside, he added an extension to bring in guest rooms, a work space, and a room large enough to be used as a cinema.

the Beatles rarely carried cash, preferring to have stores bill them when needed. This proved embarrassing when they were visiting the Maharishi in Wales, without their manager, and ate late at a Chinese restaurant. After exchanging nervous glances and realizing what they had gotten into, George went into his reserves—a wad of ten-pound notes hidden in his sandal sole.

ringo had perhaps even more of an aversion to cash than the other Beatles. He claimed that he has never carried cash, and even though they all were given checkbooks early in their careers, he said he has never written a check. Stores where he shops, even if for the first time, seem to trust to send the bill to his accountant: "No one's ever asked me yet to prove that I really am Ringo."

by 1965, all the Beatles had upgraded their cars. George bought an E-Type Jaguar, but later traded it for an Aston-Martin, a similar model to the one Paul had. Ringo opted for an Italian car, a Facel Vega. John owned three cars: a Rolls-Royce, a Ferrari, and a Mini. He still didn't know how to drive when he made the purchases.

tours

the third national tour, which they headlined with Roy Orbison, was the first marked by minor riots. Fans who heard that George loved jelly babies (soft, gelatin-based candy similar to Gummi Bears) threw handfuls at the stage, and the band was mobbed as they entered and left the tour bus.

Although the Beatles were Roy Orbison fans, they still asked to close the show. Orbison recalled: "I was earning three times their money. They approached me and said, 'You're making the money, let us close the show.'" After the first week of the tour, Orbison lost his top billing anyway, as the Beatles' popularity grew. The Beatles and Orbison went on to become friends, and George would later invite Orbison to join the Traveling Wilburys in 1979.

when the Beatles made their first concert dates in the U.S., the crowd of 3,000 at Washington's Union Station, having never heard of jelly babies, threw jelly beans, which proved to be much more painful projectiles. The candies rained down on them throughout their American tours. "Some of them even threw [jelly beans] in bags and they hurt like hailstones," remarked Ringo.

a serious letdown came in Paris, where the Beatles played at the Olympia Theater from January 16 to February 4, 1964. Although they had just broken the charts in America, where "I Want to Hold Your Hand" reached number one, the

97

mostly male audience in Paris was nonplussed. The *Daily Mail* wrote "Beatlemania is still, like Britain's entry into the Common Market, a problem the French prefer to put off for a while." The band wouldn't return until June 1965.

When they did, at the Palais des Sports, Paul made attempts to introduce songs in French, which brought cheers from the 6,000-seat house.

turnout for the Beatles' 1965 European tour was generally disappointing, with several stadiums less than half-full. At the Palazzo Dello Sport, Genoa, only 5,000 turned out for the afternoon show in the 25,000-seat stadium. After three Italian disappointments, the Beatles never returned.

on their first American visit, the band stayed at the Plaza Hotel in Manhattan, but when the manager found himself coping with crowds of fans, he asked on the radio if there were any other hotels interested in taking the group. On their next visit, they stayed at the Warwick, at 54th Street and Sixth Avenue.

their two Carnegie Hall concerts were attended by 6,000. Their first date, February 12, 1964, marked the first time that a rock group had appeared at the venue. Promoter Sid Bernstein arranged for extra seats on the stage after the show was sold out, but the Carnegie management only agreed to this if they went to older VIPs. Lauren Bacall and Happy Rockefeller were among those who got seats, but Bernstein had to turn down David Niven, William Zeckendorf and Shirley MacLaine. The Beatles made $9,335.78 (nearly $50,000 in 1997 currency) for the two shows.

Security at Carnegie Hall was provided by three hundred police officers.

Unfortunately for collectors, the American Federation of Musicians reportedly prevented Capitol from recording the Carnegie shows.

the record-breaking American tour started on August 19, 1964, at the Cow Palace in San Francisco. Joining the band were Jackie De Shannon, the Righteous Brothers, the Bill Black Combo, and the Exciters. The tour went on to Las Vegas, Seattle, Vancouver, Los Angeles, Denver, Cincinnati, New York, Atlantic City, Philadelphia, Indianapolis, Milwaukee, Chicago, Detroit, Toronto, Montreal, Jacksonville, Boston, Baltimore, Pittsburgh, Cleveland, New Orleans, Kansas City, and Dallas. The Beatles would cover 22,441 miles on this tour, and spend a total of sixty hours, twenty-five minutes in the air.

all 17,130 seats at the Cow Palace were sold out, and ticket sales grossed $91,670. The Beatles got $47,600 (about $250,000 in 1997 currency). Backstage, they met Joan Baez, Derek Taylor, and Shirley Temple.

in Seattle, 14,045 fans showed up. Crowd control was handled by fifty police, fourteen firemen, and one hundred navy men.

ringo said that the police at American shows fell to autograph hunting as much as the fans they were protecting the band from. One he caught going through their pockets.

in Los Angeles, the Beatles became the first rock band to perform at the Hollywood Bowl, to a crowd of 18,700. Capitol Records taped the thirty-five-minute concert, but didn't release the recording for thirteen years, when it was packaged with their two later Hollywood Bowl performances.

at Denver, the "Mile-High City," the unacclimated Beatles required hits from oxygen tanks to complete the show.

by the time they got to New York, crowd control had proven so difficult that the New York Police Department insisted that the managers of the Forest Hills Tennis Stadium allow the Beatles to be dropped off by a helicopter for their two performances.

in Atlantic City, they played before 19,000 fans at the convention center, three days after the Democratic National Convention, on a specially built 15-foot high platform. After the show, they made their getaway in a laundry truck.

at the Gator Bowl in Jacksonville, Florida, the Beatles performed in the aftermath of Hurricane Dora, and their arrival was delayed by President Johnson's departure from the same airport in Air Force One. His motorcade performed double duty, simply waiting at the airport to escort the Beatles to the George Washington Hotel.

for their Cleveland show, fans could not buy a ticket directly, but had to register their name with radio station WHK, which selected 12,000 names at random. Those selected were then allowed to buy tickets. During the performance, the Cleveland chief of police interrupted the show by shoving George away from his microphone and announcing that if anyone left their assigned seat, the show would be off.

in New Orleans, the mayor declared a "Beatles Day," and presented keys to the city to each member of the band, along with honorary citizenships. This warm welcome didn't extend to the fans, however. The New Orleans Police Department charged the fans on horseback and threatened them with nightsticks. According to Ringo, "It was like watching the police play stickball with the kids."

the contracts for shows in Southern states stipulated that the Beatles would "not be required to perform before a segregated audience."

the tour concluded with a return visit to New York, where the band played a benefit concert at the Paramount Theater on September 20. Tickets for the 3,682-seat concert sold for five to one hundred dollars, bringing in teens as well as the wealth and power of New York, and raising $25,000 for the Retarded Infants Service and Cerebral Palsy of New York. Backstage, the Beatles met Bob Dylan for the first time.

back from their first American tour, September 20, 1964, they began their biggest British tour yet with a twenty-seven-city tour from October 9 to November 10, 1964. The band got only four nights off that month.

on this tour the Beatles made their first appearance in Northern Ireland, declining their Royal Command Performance invitation, which they had received just two weeks before. With a crowd of 17,400 packed into King's Hall, Belfast, it also marked the largest crowd ever gathered for a pop show in the United Kingdom.

adelaide, the capital of South Australia, wasn't a scheduled stop on the Beatles' world tour until the Beatles' promoter received a petition signed by 80,000, asking the band to change their plans.

A problem arose when the only venue which could handle the band, Centennial Hall, increased the booking fee by seven times the normal rate. Local businesspersons managed to come up with the cash needed to change the tour dates, and the Beatles played two shows.

a similar initiative was spearheaded by the owner of the Kansas City Athletics baseball team. The businessman had seen them perform in San Francisco on their first American tour and offered Epstein $50,000 for a single performance at the Municipal Stadium. He later upped his offer to $100,000, but when he learned that this was comparable to the going rate, he offered a record-breaking fee of $150,000 (over three-quarters of a million in 1997 dollars). The Beatles lost their one day off to include Kansas City on their tour.

The Kansas City police chief was not as enthusiastic: He was heard saying that he would rather deal with an invasion from Mars than a Beatle concert and sent 350 policemen to handle the record crowd of 20,208.

the Beatles made their only Japanese appearances at the Nippon Budokan Hall in Tokyo on June 30, July 1, and July 2, 1966. The venue was considered by some a sacred place, due to the traditional, dignified martial arts exhibitions which took place there, and the Beatles received several death threats before their appearance. Accordingly, over 35,000 security men were employed during the visit to Japan, and after the shows, 3,000 police mingled with the audience of 11,000.

the Japan visit was followed by the chaotic events in Manila following their July 4, 1966, performance. When the band first arrived in Manila, they were offered a large yacht by the Philippines promoter, Ramon Ramos, near the navy base, but Epstein refused, and the band moved to the Manila Hotel. Their schedule, arranged by Ramos, stated that a three o'clock visit with Imelda Marcos and President Marcos on July 4 was optional, and the band chose not to attend, needing to be at the stadium at least two hours before the concert. Ramos, possibly embarrassed, chose not to inform the palace, which was under the impression that the Beatles would definitely visit at 11:00, and brought in 200 children to meet the band. When palace representatives arrived to find the Beatles still in bed and Epstein refusing to wake them up, they returned to the President with news not of misunderstanding, but a deliberate snub. After the show, the television news reported that the President and First Lady had been insulted. Epstein's statement and apology were read on television, but the broadcast was scrambled by interference, which went away as soon as it was over, causing the Beatles' management to think it was caused deliberately. Meanwhile, Ramos refused to pay as agreed, claiming that the band would have to pick up the entertainment tax, and got the government tax office involved, which refused to allow the band to leave without guarantee of payment. Epstein gave in just so the group could leave as planned. The police charged with protecting the Beatles were withdrawn, and the band and entourage had to fight their way through a crowd of two hundred. Epstein was punched in the face, and their chauffeur received a spine injury and a cracked rib. The airport manager shut off all the escalators as the harassed group made their way through the airport, and finally, on board the plane, they were informed that they couldn't leave due to a quickly manufactured visa problem, which delayed their flight for almost an hour. It was after this nightmare that the band reconsidered whether to tour at all.

The first Manila concert drew a crowd of 30,000, and the evening concert brought 50,000.

the final British concert took place at Wembley Stadium, just north of London, on May 1, 1966. Fans were at the time unaware that this was their last home country performance.

during their last tour of the United States, a psychic who had predicted the death of John F. Kennedy predicted that the Beatles would die in a plane crash. Several of their supporting acts refused to fly with them after this.

the second American tour kicked off at the 55,600-seat Shea Stadium, New York City, and was organized by Sid Bernstein, who had originally brought the Beatles to Carnegie Hall. The world-record audience brought in a record gross of $304,000 (about $1.5 million in 1997 dollars), and the Beatles received $160,000 for one night's performance. However, after paying for the venue, not to mention the $25,000 bill from Lloyd's of London for insurance, Bernstein's share was $6,500 (over $30,000 in today's currency).

Opening acts included Brenda Holloway, the King Curtis Band, Sounds Incorporated, and Cannibal and the Headhunters. Ed Sullivan introduced the Beatles to the Shea Stadium crowd.

Sullivan Productions, with Subafilm Ltd., filmed the Shea Stadium concert, and the fifty-minute film aired on the BBC on March 1, 1966.

The Beatles' return to Shea Stadium on August 23, 1966, brought them an even larger fee—$189,000—even though there were 12,000 fewer fans.

when the group flew into Houston for their August 19, 1965, show, fans broke through the airport gates and swarmed around the plane as it taxied down the runway. Epstein and the Beatles were extracted from the plane by forklift.

the best-attended Beatles concert of the final tour was at Dodger Stadium, Los Angeles, on August 28, 1966. Forty-five thousand fans packed the stands, and after the show the police charged the crowd with shields out and clubs overhead. The fans retaliated by throwing bottles and sticks, and attempted to break down the 150-foot gates with the wooden barricades intended to keep them back.

in Cincinnati, the promoter failed to provide a canopy over the stage, and the show was canceled by rain just before the band was due to go on. Thirty-five thousand fans had to be turned away, and were given tickets to the next day's show.

the rain didn't stop the performance in St. Louis, Missouri, but the misery of performing under a corrugated iron shelter to a crowd that was "miles away," getting soaked, and the worry of water getting onto the electrical equipment finally convinced Paul, the last holdout, that touring should end.

the final Beatles concert was held at Candlestick Park, San Francisco, on August 29, 1966. They had not yet announced that this would be their last tour, and 20,000 seats went unsold. Their first song of the evening was "Rock and Roll Music," and they closed with "Long Tall Sally." Both George and Ringo took turns at lead vocal, with Ringo singing "I Wanna Be Your Man," and George singing his own composition, "If I Needed Someone."

A tape of the last concert was made by Tony Barrow, a Beatles public relations worker, at Paul's request. Barrow had Sotheby's auction the tape in 1988, and a bootleg album of the last concert started circulating shortly afterward.

although they had just finished recording *Revolver,* no songs from this album made it onto the playlist of their last tour.

by the end of their touring days, the Beatles had played a total of 1,400 concerts.

friends and influences

neil Aspinall started working for the Beatles in 1961, when he bought a van and charged them five shillings (a quarter of a pound) per person to take the band to various gigs. He remained their most loyal friend and assistant throughout their careers, served as road manager, and eventually became managing director of Apple Corps. He has remained silent about his personal experiences with the band, and claims that if he ever wrote a book about his life with the Beatles, he would only have it published after his death.

george's ex-wife, Patti Boyd, is generally credited with inspiring the Beatles' interest in Hindu spirituality, introducing the Beatles to Maharishi Mahesh Yogi at his lecture at the Hilton Hotel in London on August 24, 1967.

after the release of *Sgt. Pepper's Lonely Hearts Club Band,* Timothy Leary made this comment on the Beatles' otherworldly origins: "I declare that the Beatles are mutants. Prototypes of evolutionary agents sent by God with a mysterious power to create a new species—a young race of laughing freemen. . . . They are the wisest, holiest, most effective avatars the human race has ever produced."

the Beatles met the Rolling Stones in April 1963, when the Stones' unofficial manager invited them to the Crawdaddy Club, London, where the up-and-coming band was performing. The Beatles loved the performance, and the audience's reaction, and went back to their place after the show. They then invited the Stones to their Royal Albert Hall performance, and three of them showed up. After the Stones were signed to Decca Records, critics invariably compared them to the Beatles, saying that the Stones were the rebellious alternative to the clean-cut fab four. Ironically, as many commentators have remarked, the Stones all went to middle-class schools while the Beatles had cultivated a rough, working-class image in Hamburg and Liverpool before Brian Epstein came along. The message "Welcome Rolling Stones" appears on the front cover of *Sgt. Pepper,* while the Stones have a photo of the Beatles on the *Their Satanic Majesties Request* album.

the Stones and the Beatles used to agree not to release their singles and albums at the same time, giving each other enough space so as to not prevent either or both from reaching number one in the charts.

although they were influenced by each other's music, the Beatles and the Beach Boys didn't meet until August 22, 1965, when Carl Wilson and Mike Love visited them at their Portland concert. The Beatles contacted them later during the Beach Boys' first U.K. tour.

brian Wilson was amazed when he heard the *Rubber Soul* album: "I was sitting around a table with friends, making a joint when we heard *Rubber Soul* for the first time, and I'm smoking and getting high and the album blew my mind." *Rubber Soul* became an inspiration for *Pet Sounds,* which in turn became an inspiration for *Sgt. Pepper's Lonely Hearts Club Band.*

paul called the Beach Boys' "God Only Knows" the best song ever written, and the Beach Boys played the opening party for *Magical Mystery Tour.* Mike Love also joined the band at the Maharishi's ashram in India.

john listed his favorite contemporary musicians in an interview: the Byrds, the Lovin' Spoonful, and the Mamas and the Papas.

peter Sellers performed at the Beatles' invitation for their TV special *The Music of Lennon and McCartney* in 1965. Dressed as Richard III, he did a version of "A Hard Day's Night" with Shakespearean overtones. Sellers and Ringo became good friends during the filming of *The Magic Christian,* and eventually the comedian sold Ringo his estate, Brookfield, for a cut-rate price. Sellers had recorded with George Martin even before the Beatles came along, and after their success, he recorded hilarious spoken-word versions of "She Loves You" and "Can't Buy Me Love" in 1965.

eric Clapton met George Harrison when he was with the Yardbirds, playing a Christmas show with the Beatles. Eric and George kept up their friendship as Eric became guitarist for Cream, and worked with George on the *Wonderwall* album. Eric also joined John in the Plastic Ono Band. Eric eventually married George's ex-wife, Patti, but their friendship remained intact.

john credited Bob Dylan with awakening him to new lyrical possibilities. In 1964, he remarked, "I was not too keen on lyrics in those days. I didn't think they counted. Dylan used to come out with his latest acetate and say, 'Listen to the words, man,' and I'd say, 'I don't listen to words.' " John later credited him in his lyrics to "Yer Blues," with a line that says he feels like Dylan's Mr. Jones, a reference to Dylan's "Ballad of a Thin Man."

paul took an interest in the philosopher Bertrand Russell, who was then active in the peace movement, and went to meet the ninety-two-year-old activist at his home. Paul says Russell was the first one to make him aware of the situation in Vietnam.

in August 1965 the Beatles rented a house at 2850 Benedict Canyon in Los Angeles with views of the Hollywood Hills and a swimming pool. At this address they were visited by Joan Baez, the Byrds, Jane Fonda, Rock Hudson, and Dick Van

Dyke. Local radio stations let fans know the exact address, and besides the expected throngs watching the house with binoculars, a group of die-hard fans rented a helicopter for fly-overs.

it was during this stay that the Beatles made their visit to Elvis Presley, who John credited as his main inspiration: "Nothing really affected me until I heard Elvis. If there hadn't been Elvis, there would not have been the Beatles." When they arrived on August 27, 1965, it took some time for the superstars to get comfortable. Presley finally said, "Look guys, if you're just going to sit and stare at me, then I'm going to bed." They instead broke out guitars and amplifiers, and Paul instructed Elvis on the bass, which he was just learning. While Paul says that the sessions were captured on tape, George insists they were not.

among the students at the Maharishi's ashram was singer Donovan, who became close to the Beatles over the next few years. Paul and George saw him perform at the Royal Albert Hall in January 1967, and the entire band went to see him at the Saville Theatre later that year. He received some sitar lessons from George. Paul is rumored to have contributed his voice to the chorus of Donovan's "Mellow Yellow."

DRUG USE

according to Paul, while John and Stuart were in art school, they would extract the Benzedrine from inhalers to get high.

in Hamburg, when they were performing all day and late into the night, the band learned from German patrons that diet pills could keep them going. They later took on stronger pills, such as "Black Bombers" and "Purple Hearts."

the Beatles first used marijuana on August 28, 1964, when Bob Dylan offered it to them while visiting them at the Delmonico Hotel in New York. After securing the room, drawing all the curtains, and placing towels under the doors, they were ready. Ringo was first, and took the whole joint to himself, unaware that he was supposed to pass it on. Dylan prepared another six joints. Paul said of the occasion: "I was thinking for the first time. Really thinking."

bob Dylan heard the line "I can't hide" in "I Want to Hold Your Hand" as "I get high" and was only corrected when he met the Beatles for the first time.

john and George were first given LSD, without their knowledge, by a dentist friend in 1965. John recalled, "The first time we took acid was really an accident. Me and George were at dinner and someone gave it to us when we didn't know much about it. We'd taken pot, but that was all. We hadn't heard of the horrors of LSD. And we weren't supervised, which you should be. We did think we were going barmy."

The LSD was slipped into their coffee cups via a sugar

cube after dinner. George recalled, "It was as if we suddenly found ourselves in the middle of a horror film. The room seemed to get bigger and bigger. Our host seemed to change into a demon. We were all terrified."

But in 1987, he painted a different picture: "Up until LSD, I never realized that there was anything beyond this normal waking state of consciousness. . . . The first time I took it, it just blew everything away. I had such an incredible feeling of well-being, that there was a God and I could see him in every blade of grass. It was like gaining hundreds of years' experience within twelve hours. It changed me and there was no way back to what I was before. It wasn't all good, though, because it left quite a lot of questions as well."

John reflected on his intense LSD use in 1970: "[Acid] went on for years. I must have had a thousand trips. I used to just eat it all the time."

the Beatles claim they generally only used marijuana in the studio, and not every time. They typically didn't bring drink into their workspace, and only once did John, accidentally, take acid during a studio session.

in 1966, Paul first experimented with LSD with his friend Tara Browne, a Guinness heir. His second time was on March 21, 1967, while the band was working on *Sgt. Pepper*. John had embarked on his accidental trip, and Paul, who took him back to his place, decided to join him.

Paul admitted to using LSD to *Life* magazine. "It opened my eyes," he told their interviewer. "We only use one-tenth of our brains. Just think what we'd accomplish if we could tap that hidden part." The supposedly strait-laced Brian Epstein would shock the establishment by admitting to taking LSD as well shortly afterwards.

The Beatles were equally surprised, but began to party with their manager on a new level. They kicked things off with a big party at Kingsley Hill, where Winston Churchill had held war council meetings with the Chiefs of Staff. Cynthia joined the mass trip, her first time since the dentist incident, and the aftereffects and nightmares reportedly drove her to contemplate suicide.

In 1968 Paul backed down slightly on his enthusiasm for LSD: "I don't recommend [acid]. It can open a few doors, but it's not any answer. You go out and get the answers yourself."

paul said he experimented with cocaine for about a year, starting from around the time of the *Sgt. Pepper* sessions.

john was an admitted user of heroin, although he denied injecting it. He said he eventually quit.

in 1967, after the Rolling Stones' Keith Richard and Mick Jagger had been jailed and fined for marijuana possession, the Beatles sponsored an ad in the London *Times* supporting cannabis law reform. The Beatles, David Hockney, R. D. Laing, Francis Huxley, Graham Greene, Nobel Laureate Francis Crick, Brian Epstein, and M.P. Tom Driberg, among sixty-five others, lent their names to the ad.

The day the advertisement appeared, it was condemned in the British Parliament by the minister of state, who specifically commented on Paul's remarks to the press about the influence of LSD on his religious beliefs.

in spring 1968, the Beatles announced that they had given up drugs. They hadn't.

george Martin, while compiling comments for a television show on the making of *Sgt. Pepper,* asked Paul what was the driving force behind the album. Paul replied "Drugs. Pot," and shocked Martin further by confirming that they were on drugs the entire time.

on October 18, 1968, John and Yoko were arrested for possession of cannabis. They were picked up at Ringo's flat in Montagu Square, where seven officers and a drug-sniffing dog searched the premises and found one and a half ounces of marijuana. They were booked at the Marylebone police station, and later released on bail to a crowd of three hundred outside the station. The trial was set for November 27. John pleaded guilty and cleared Yoko of any connection to the drugs found. He was fined 150 pounds.

on March 12, 1969, the day of Paul's marriage to Linda, police raided George Harrison's house in Esher and found over an ounce of marijuana. George, who was visiting a friend during the raid, returned home to find his wife calmly sitting with the officers, watching television and listening to records.

Patti had told them where to find the pot after the drug sniffing dog, Yogi, had found a block of hash. According to Patti, later that night at a party, George approached Lord Snowdon to see if he could stop the raid. "I was casually looking around, when suddenly I spotted my younger sister Paula puffing on a joint which she then proceeded to offer Princess Margaret . . . I couldn't believe it, it was the early evening of the same day that we'd just been busted and there was my sister trying to hand Princess Margaret a joint!"

paul's opinions on the legal status of marijuana have continued to be public and vehement. In a 1997 *New Statesman* interview, he repeated his belief that marijuana should be decriminalized.

INDIAN INFLUENCES

one month after the final Beatles tour, in September 1966, George left for India with his wife, cultivating what would become a lifelong interest in Indian spirituality and music. He had met the Indian musician Ravi Shankar and spiritual leader Maharishi Mahesh Yogi in June of 1966. George traveled to India in the fall for two months of Shankar's sitar lessons, and became obsessed with the instrument and the new possibilities of Indian music.

the Beatles, accompanied by Mick Jagger and Marianne Faithfull, traveled by train from London to Bangor, a small town in Wales where the Maharishi had a spiritual center, on August 25, 1967. This was their first trip made without Brian Epstein and their road managers since their rise to fame. John said it felt like "going somewhere without your trousers." The entire town came out for their arrival, with the usual screaming teenagers standing alongside older and more curious townspeople.

The Beatles left the meditation center when they learned of Brian Epstein's death. The Maharishi attempted to comfort them by placing his death in spiritual perspective.

john and George, with their wives, flew to Delhi on February 15, 1968 to attend the Maharishi Mahesh Yogi's three-month transcendental meditation course at his ashram, the Academy of Meditation at Shankaracharya Nagar, India. They were joined by Ringo and Paul, with Maureen Starkey and Jane Asher, on February 19. Also in attendance for the course were Cynthia Lennon, Patti Harrison, Jennie Boyd, Mia Farrow, the Beatles' friend Alexis Mardas, Donovan, the Beach Boys' Mike Love, and jazzman Paul Horn. All attendees wore traditional Indian dress at the ashram—saris for women, kurta tunics and sandals for men. John briefly wore a turban.

donovan said that he gave John lessons on folk-oriented finger-style guitar playing while at the ashram, which allowed John to write "Julia" and "Dear Prudence" based on the picking he had learned.

george and John were the Beatles' most avid meditators, meditating for seven to nine hours a day during their stay at the ashram. Ringo, however, couldn't adjust to the food, and his wife was troubled by insects, so they left early. Paul and Jane Asher were the next to go, after being in the ashram for six weeks, and explained when they got back that they had been homesick.

george and John remained enthralled by the Maharishi until Mardas eventually presented them with enough evidence of his supposed greed and hypocrisy that they decided to leave. When they told the spiritual leader they were leaving, and he asked why, John quipped, "You're the cosmic one. You ought to know."

the Maharishi, before the Beatles had arrived at Rishikesh, had repeatedly promised ABC a television special with himself and the Beatles, without asking their permission. When Paul and George confronted him, he merely gave them one of his characteristic giggles.

the weeks spent at the ashram and the positive and negative experiences with the Maharishi were responsible for an incredible outpouring of material, over forty songs. With only a few exceptions, all of the songs on *Abbey Road* and the White Album were written at, or found inspiration from, the time the Beatles spent at the ashram.

the song "Sexy Sadie" was originally about the Maharishi, and mentioned him by name, but when it was recorded, Lennon decided against recording an exposé and changed "Maharishi" to "Sexy Sadie."

"**the** Fool on the Hill" similarly was Paul "writing about someone like Maharishi."

banned beatles

the BBC banned "Lucy in the Sky with Diamonds" due to the supposed LSD reference.

"a Day in the Life" was banned by BBC for supposed references to drug use, contained in the line about smoking and going into a dream. The image of someone blowing his mind out in a car was another point of contention, and track marks from IV drug use were seen in the line about four thousand holes in Blackburn, Lancashire.

in the United States, a censorship campaign was started by Governor Spiro T. Agnew, who quoted the line "I get high with a little help from my friends." The John Birch Society declared that the Beatles were Communists and the *Sgt. Pepper* album proved "an understanding of the principles of brainwashing."

"come Together" was banned for its reference to Coca-Cola, which was determined by the BBC to be advertising.

the BBC deemed "Happiness Is a Warm Gun" to be full of sexual references, and banned it from the radio. Others speculated that the song was about intravenous drug use.

"I Am the Walrus" felt the BBC censor's ax due to "indecent" references, including "knickers" and "yellow-matter custard."

beatles on tv

one of the Beatles' earliest breaks was a 1963 appearance on *Thank Your Lucky Stars,* seen by millions throughout Britain.

on December 7, 1963, the Beatles wrapped up two TV appearances, first for *Juke Box Jury,* a program in which current celebrities listened to and commented on the week's singles. The Beatles heard ten songs by artists such as Elvis Presley, The Swinging Blue Jeans, Billy Fury, Shirley Ellis, and the Merseybeats. The special edition of the show was broadcast from the Empire Theatre, Liverpool, and was seen by 23 million viewers.

the same night, they taped their first TV special, *It's the Beatles,* a thirty-minute performance for 2,500 members of the Northern Area Fan Club. They then dashed off to the Odeon, just down the road, for another concert. The special aired that same evening.

in 1964, the band appeared in another of their own TV specials, *Around the Beatles.* Filmed over two days in April, it was broadcast on May 6, and featured, in addition to a dozen songs, a sketch of the Beatles in costume acting out a segment of *A Midsummer Night's Dream.*

epstein arranged the appearances on *The Ed Sullivan Show* for the Beatles, although Sullivan at first refused to give the band top billing. They agreed on February 9 and 16, 1964, and the Beatles reportedly received $3,500 for each show, plus another $3,000 for a taped performance to be used later. The viewing audience for the first show was a record-breaking seventy-three million. News stations reported that juvenile crime was virtually nonexistent that night.

sullivan had a brush with Beatlemania before Epstein's visit, when his landing at Heathrow was delayed by the crowds greeting the band on their return from Sweden.

brian Epstein reportedly asked Sullivan on the night of the first performance, "I would like to know the exact wording of your introduction." Sullivan replied, "I would like you to get lost."

the Beatles received a telegram of congratulations from Elvis Presley, which was read on the air.

the *Ed Sullivan Show,* which only had space for 728 in its studio, received over 50,000 ticket requests for the two dates.

as the camera panned each member of the band, type appeared at the bottom of the screen with their first names. Under John's name was the message, "Sorry girls, he's married."

when the Beatles returned to *The Ed Sullivan Show* for an August 14, 1965, appearance, their viewing audience matched their earlier record-setting audience.

the Beatles were interviewed by telephone on *American Bandstand* on February 15, 1964. They never appeared live on the show, but there was one installment in 1964 dedicated entirely to the Beatles.

after a two-year break from performances on regular television programs, the Beatles appeared on *The David Frost Show* in 1968, performing "Hey Jude" at Twickenham Studios.

beatles on film

paul, who was engaged in avant-garde filmmaking in the late sixties, and was the driving force behind *Magical Mystery Tour,* prophesied the rise of the music video: "In the future all records will have vision as well as sound. In twenty years' time people will be amazed to think we just listened to records."

on December 22, 1963, an eight-minute film, *The Beatles Come to Town,* started screening as part of the Pathé News newsreel. It featured the Beatles performing "She Loves You" and "Twist and Shout" at the Apollo Theater in Ardwick, Manchester.

A HARD DAY'S NIGHT

the band made its first movie deal in late 1963, with United Artists. Paul had earlier suggested Alun Owen, a Liverpool-based writer of several major teleplays, for the script. Owen went on to write *A Hard Day's Night,* which was nominated for an Oscar for best screenplay.

the Beatles still had not convinced the money men in the States of their staying power, and United Artists wanted the movie to be as cheap as possible. Shooting the film in black and white, which was against the producer's original wishes, was one way they cut corners.

the band started shooting *A Hard Day's Night* in March 1964. The film, budgeted at under £200,000, was directed by Dick Lester, who had worked with Peter Sellers and Spike Milligan. Much of the filming was done on the London streets, with the expected crowd scenes that followed the Beatles everywhere working their way into the final cut. Once, a small crowd even chased a messenger who was taking film cans back to the studio, causing him to drop several rolls.

the film premiered in London's West End in July 1965. Among the guests to the after-show party were Princess Margaret and Lord Snowdon. No one expected them to show up—their invitation was a formality—but they made an appearance for drinks.

foreign distributors found the near-nonsensical title difficult to translate, and came up with titles like *Tutti per Uno,* Italian for "all for one," or *Quatre Garçons dans le Vent,* French for "four boys in the wind." In Germany it was released as *Yeah Yeah Yeah die Beatles,* and in the Netherlands as *Yeah Yeah Yeah Darr de Beatles.*

the *Village Voice* called it "the *Citizen Kane* of jukebox movies," and it went on to gross 14 million dollars in its first release (around $55 million in 1997 dollars). This placed it among the best-attended movies of the time.

filming for *Help!* started on February 23, 1965, in Nassau, the Bahamas. The location then changed to Austria for the famous skiing scenes. Interior scenes were shot at Twickenham Studios, Surrey, the studio the band had used for *A Hard Day's Night*. Once again, United Artists was distributor, Dick Lester was director, and Walter Shenson was producer. The script was written by Marc Behm and Christopher Wood, and involves a series of fantastic adventures surrounding a ring with magical powers stuck on Ringo's finger. The film cost $1.5 million, and opened at the London Pavilion on July 29, 1965. The premiere raised six thousand pounds for the Docklands settlement and the Variety Club Heart Fund.

in one scene, the Beatles sing Beethoven's "Ode to Joy" to calm a lion. Off camera was a lion tamer with a rifle at ready.

other cast members included Eleanor Bron, John Bluthal, Warren Mitchell, Peter Copely, Dandy Nichols, Bruce Lacey, and Mal Evans. Eleanor Bron, who played a mystical Eastern princess who saves the Beatles from trouble, became friends with John Lennon, and held long conversations with him in the hotel bar. They met again when the Beatles played the Hollywood Bowl.

the soundtrack for *Help!* used a sitar, which caught George Harrison's attention. He soon bought one and started to learn Indian music. The sitar was featured prominently on the next Beatles album, *Rubber Soul.*

although not as well-reviewed as *A Hard Day's Night, Help!* won first prize at the International Film Festival in Rio de Janeiro, where it was the official British entry, and the *Daily Express* compared the band to the Marx Brothers.

the Beatles were required by contract to do three films, but the third was a long time coming as the band rejected one script after another. At one point, they bought rights to a Western script entitled *A Talent for Loving,* only to reject it later. They also considered a comedy version of *The Three Musketeers,* with Brigitte Bardot in the role of Lady De Winter.

YELLOW SUBMARINE

thinking that an animated feature would satisfy their contract, the Beatles reluctantly agreed to *Yellow Submarine,* originally conceived by Al Brodax, animated by George Dunning, directed by Charles Jenkins, and designed by Heinz Edelmann. The script was credited to Lee Minoff, Al Brodax, Jack Mendlesohn, and Erich Segal, and Heinz Edelmann claims there were at least twenty scripts. Roger McGough, a Liverpool poet, was brought in to add local color to the dialogue, and was not credited. Erich Segal, a professor of Greek and Latin at Yale University, received most of the press attention. Erich Segal went on to write bestselling romantic novels.

true to the subtitle—*Nothing is Real*—the Beatles' voices were supplied by actors. They appear for real only at the end of the film.

MAGICAL MYSTERY TOUR

paul got the idea for *Magical Mystery Tour* from reading about Ken Kesey and the Merry Pranksters, who were traveling around the United States in a psychedelic bus, spreading the hippie gospel and proclaiming the benefits of LSD. It was discussed with Brian Epstein before his death, but filming started after he died, in September 1967.

the actors were all asked to improvise, and non-structure was the rule of thumb. However, Paul called himself the director, more or less: "I think it was generally considered that I was directing it." Ringo is credited as director of photography.

what would be filmed day by day was left mostly to chance. John woke up one morning after having had a dream that he was a waiter piling pasta on a patron. Paul had this idea filmed

with John using a shovel to serve spaghetti to an obese
woman.

the film revolves around a bus trip taken by the band with
thirty-nine others, including fan club officials, film crew, and
various members of the Beatles' inner circle. The bus left
London on September 11, 1967, and the tour finished on
September 15.

the band had originally planned to make one stop every
night, but by the time they reached Newquay, Cornwall, this
idea was dropped, and they stayed in one location, filming
for three days.

other filming took place in the West Malling Royal Air
Force Station, Paul Raymond's Revue Bar in London, and
Nice, France, where Paul completed his "Fool on the Hill"
scene.

for the sequence for "Flying," Paul contacted his friend Dennis O'Dell, who had worked on *Dr. Strangelove,* and was given
unused aerial footage from the final scene in the movie, which
takes place over northern Russia. To make the shots look
new rather than recycled, the film was tinted.

editing the ten hours of footage down to fifty-three minutes took eleven weeks, and the final cost of the film was £40,000, around $100,000. The Beatles sold the broadcast rights to the BBC for £9,000. Paul says he could have got more from another source, but wanted the film to go out on a nation-wide broadcast.

the show aired on BBC 2 on Boxing Day, December 26, 1967, to an audience of between thirteen and fifteen million. The critics were unforgiving. The *Daily Express* called it "blatant rubbish" and "tasteless nonsense." Negotiations with the American networks broke down in the wake of the critical onslaught.

paul appeared on *The David Frost Show* for damage control. He stood by the film, but admitted that having it air on one of the biggest family viewing days of the year, just after most homes in Britain had finished their Christmas dinner, was a mistake.

in May 1968, it played to special screenings in Los Angeles and San Francisco, and premiered months later at Boston's Savoy Theater. In America, *Magical Mystery Tour* went on to gross two million dollars just from college rentals.

the launch party for *Magical Mystery Tour* demanded fancy dress. George Martin came as the Duke of Edinburgh, Patti Martin went as a belly dancer, and John came as a Teddy Boy.

LET IT BE

this project was originally conceived as a television documentary on the making of a Beatles album, tied to the release of the tentatively titled album *Get Back,* which became *Let It Be.* Although strains in the Beatles' relationship were beginning to show, they still had the three-film obligation to United Artists, and began filming their recording sessions at Twickenham Studios on January 2, 1969. They wrapped up with ninety-six hours of film, which took a year to edit, on January 17. At this point the idea of editing the footage down to a TV documentary was scrapped.

the Beatles recorded over thirty hours of music—over one hundred songs—during the filming, most of them covers or traditional favorites. Most have still not been released.

george was frustrated with the band's relationships during this time, walking out for several days after expressing discontent with Paul's instructions. He was also absolutely against the idea of returning to public performances, which Paul was attempting to push. He did, however, agree to the final rooftop concert, which appears in the film.

one of the best-remembered images from the film was the one of the last Beatles performance, on top of the Apple Corps headquarters at 3 Savile Row, London. The performance was held on January 30, 1969, and was scheduled to last forty-two minutes. The crowds below completely stopped traffic, and the police received numerous complaints.

there was a plan to have actors dressed as policemen rudely interrupting the rooftop concert, but when the real police showed up, they were so polite that the director felt it would be unfair to represent them as planned. *Rolling Stone* critic Michael Goodwin, however, didn't believe that the police were real, citing the sophisticated editing of the footage that showed them entering the building.

the film was directed by Michael Lindsay-Hogg, who was criticized by reviewers, and especially by *Rolling Stone*. The *Morning Star* was also particularly harsh: "For those who expected it to throw some light on the development of the Beatles phenomenon, it is disappointedly barren." However, the film won an Oscar in 1970 for Best Original Song Score.

yoko appears in the film, as mentioned by the *Evening Standard*: "Yoko passes by like Lady Macbeth sleepwalking." The *Daily Mirror* reviewer wrote that she "sits broodingly at her husband's elbow throughout, looking like an inscrutable miniature Mother Earth."

john called the filming and studio time "the most miserable session on earth."

however, all the Beatles seemed to enjoy the rooftop performance, which would be their last performance in public.

solo and side ventures

it was on their first national tour that Lennon and McCartney started writing songs for other artists, including "Misery" for Helen Shapiro, which was declined by her record company. They later wrote "Bad to Me" for Billy J. Kramer, which became a number one single in the U.K., and "I'll Keep You Satisfied," which went to number four.

while living with the Asher family, Paul helped launch the careers of folksingers Peter Asher and Gordon Waller with the song "A World Without Love," which went to the top of the charts in America and displaced the Beatles' "Can't Buy Me Love" from number one in Britain.

in 1965 the American production company King Features started a Saturday morning cartoon based on the Beatles and featuring their songs. The cartoon, which ran for sixty-seven episodes from September 25, 1965, received no input from the band. However, the executive producer, Al Brodax, would later become a key figure in the *Yellow Submarine* animated feature. The recurring theme of the series was the Beatles dodging their fans.

john accepted a part in *How I Won the War,* directed by Dick Lester, in 1966, and went to Spain to act in the film after the Beatles' final tour. The film was released in 1967, and John soon began making experimental films with Yoko, a partnership which would, over the years, bring films such as *Imagine, The One to One Concert, Ten For Two, Erection, Apotheosis, Up Your Legs, Fly, Self-Portrait, Honeymoon, Rape,* and *Two Virgins.*

ringo, while still with the Beatles, appeared in a number of feature films. In *Candy,* based on the novel by Terry Southern and Mason Hoffenberg, and featuring Richard Burton and Marlon Brando, Ringo plays a Mexican gardener, a very short bit part, who attempts to seduce Candy Christian, played by Swedish actress Ewa Aulin. Released in 1968, the movie received an X rating.

ringo next appeared as co-star with Peter Sellers in another adaptation of a Terry Southern novel, *The Magic Christian,* directed by Joseph McGrath and produced by the head of Apple Films, Dennis O'Dell. Raquel Welch, Roman Polanski, Spike Milligan, Christopher Lee, John Cleese, and Richard Attenborough also appear in the film. Ringo's part as Youngman Grand, adopted son of Sir Guy Grand (Peter Sellers), is not in the book and was written specially for Ringo. Paul wrote the film's theme song, "Come and Get It," which was performed by Badfinger. The song went to number four in the U.K. charts, number one in the U.S.

in the Western spoof *Blindman,* Ringo plays the bad guy, opposite Tony Anthony, who plays a blind gunfighter. Released in 1971, the film also received an X rating in Britain. The plot involves the theft of fifty women who were intended for fifty Texas miners by a Mexican desperado, and the hunting of that desperado by the blind gunslinger.

ringo played both Larry the Dwarf and Frank Zappa in Zappa's *200 Motels,* directed by Tony Palmer, who reportedly later distanced himself from the movie and refused the director's credit. The film opened in the U.S. in November 1971, but was not widely distributed in the United Kingdom.

paul began making experimental films in 1966, inspired by Jane Asher. Titled *The Defeat of the Dog* and *The Next Spring Then,* they were described by *Punch* journalist Patrick Skene as "not like ordinary people's home movies. There were overexposures, double exposures, blinding orange lights, quick cuts from professional wrestling to a crowded car-park to a close-up of a television weather map. . . . The accompanying music, on a record player and faultlessly synchronized, was by the Modern Jazz Quartet and Bach."

most of Paul's association with film has to do with film scores. In 1967 he wrote the score for *The Family Way.* After the Beatles, he would go on to write the music for the James Bond film *Live and Let Die* (1973), which earned him a Grammy and an Oscar nomination.

aside from his film scores, George Harrison started Handmade Films, one of the few bright spots in British Cinema during the late 1970s and 1980s. He started the company when Monty Python was unable to get EMI to produce their *Life of Brian,* due to their comic take on the life of Jesus. Handmade went on to produce *The Long Good Friday, Time Bandits, The Missionary, Privates on Parade, Water,* and *A Private Function.*

in 1963, Paul and John were asked to write the score for a ballet, *Mods and Rockers,* which opened on December 18, 1963, and ran to January 11, 1964, at the Prince Charles Theater in London. In their review, the *Sunday Times* called them the "greatest composers since Beethoven."

john's first book, *In His Own Write,* was published in March 1964, and displaced the latest James Bond book from the top of the bestseller lists. The *Times Literary Supplement* said it was "worth the attention of anyone who fears for the impoverishment of the English language and the British imagination." A radio interviewer praised John's prose and asked him if he made conscious use of onomatopoeia. "Automatic pier?" John replied, "I don't know what you're on about, son."

when writing the song "Woman" for Peter & Gordon, Paul McCartney used the pen name "Bernard Webb," curious about how the song would be received without the name "McCartney" attached. He was more tongue-in-cheek with his alias for his production credit on "I'm the Urban Space-man" by the Bonzo Dog Doo Dah Band, going by "Apollo C. Vermouth."

george Harrison took on an offer to do the soundtrack for the movie *Wonderwall* in January 1968. He wrote scores for both the British and Indian musicians, who use very different notation. The soundtrack was the first album release from Apple Records.

george also worked with Eric Clapton on the song "Badge" for Cream, released in April 1969. It went into the Top Twenty in the U.K., but only reached number sixty in the American singles charts. One instrumental section was borrowed by George for his composition "Here Comes the Sun."

in 1968 John and Yoko started collaborating on a series of art "happenings." They made a sculpture out of a pair of acorns, labeled "John by Yoko Ono" and "Yoko by John Lennon," and attempted to bury them at the National Sculpture Exhibition, located at Coventry Cathedral. They were informed when they arrived that they could not dig on the hallowed grounds of the Cathedral. Yoko also inspired John's first exhibition, held at the Robert Fraser Gallery. John's show consisted of charity collection boxes, among them an upsidedown hat with the message, "For the artist. Thank you." The show was dedicated "To Yoko from John with love."

in November 1968, Apple released John and Yoko's first album, *Unfinished Music No. 1—Two Virgins*. The sleeve showed the pair fully nude, and EMI refused to distribute the record. In a meeting over the album sleeve, Sir Joseph Lockwood, chairman of EMI, reportedly recommended to John and Yoko that they "find some better bodies to put on the cover than your two. They're not very attractive."

distribution was handled by Track Records, who distributed the Who, but all the albums went out in brown paper wrappers, and a shipment was seized by the police in Newark, New Jersey.

in September 1970, just before the break-up, John joined Yoko, Eric Clapton, Klaus Voorman, and Alan White on

disputes and conflicts

ringo threatened to leave the band while they were taping the White Album, and walked out of the studio for over a week. When he returned, his drum set was covered in flowers.

tensions in the studio were captured on film in *Let It Be*. According to Harrison: "There's a scene where Paul and I are having an argument . . . and we're trying to cover it up. Then the next scene I'm not there, and Yoko's just screaming, doing her screeching number. Well, that's where I'd left." George went away for several days, and recorded with other musicians. When he returned, he felt more confident, but still felt Paul was belittling him.

after John and Yoko's car accident, Yoko was under doctor's orders to stay in bed, but since John felt he needed her with him at all times, he had a bed brought into Abbey Road studios. He also had a microphone rigged above her head so he could hear her if she needed or wanted to say anything. The other Beatles were baffled and antagonized.

on September 20, 1970, Paul proposed a final move to keep the band together. They would go back on tour, appearing unannounced in small clubs, wearing disguises. Ringo liked the idea, and George didn't dismiss it. John, however, told Paul that he wanted a divorce, "like my divorce from Cynthia." He had expressed this sentiment earlier to Allen Klein, who advised him to keep it quiet until he worked out negotiations with Capitol, and now John made no formal announcement.

there was a dispute surrounding the release date of *Let It Be,* as Paul had a solo album ready for release and was asked to delay his release date until after the last Beatles album was out. Ringo, the only one still on good terms with Paul, was sent to his house to attempt to convince him out of his initial refusal. "To my dismay," he reported, "he went completely out of control, shouting at me, prodding his fingers toward my face, saying 'I'll finish you all now' and 'You'll pay.' He told me to put my coat on and get out." When Paul released his solo album, at the date he wanted, he also announced that he was leaving the band.

in press copies of his first solo album, Paul included a completed questionnaire given to him by Peter Brown of Apple. Paul was generally as vague about whether the Beatles were actually finished as John had been, saying that he didn't know whether the Beatles break-up would be temporary or permanent. However, to the question "Do you foresee a time when Lennon/McCartney becomes an active songwriting partnership again?" Paul answered, "No."

this move by Paul was taken by the press as confirmation that the band had split, and although John had made the first move, Paul was blamed as the one who finished it off. The Beatles biographer, Hunter Davies, who was friendly with Paul and Linda, soon came to the conclusion in a *Sunday Times* article that all the blame was on Yoko's shoulders. "The rest of the Beatles didn't matter anymore" to John after the arrival of Yoko, Davies wrote.

the last Beatles press release was sent out on April 10, 1970, and read: "Spring is here and Leeds play Chelsea tomorrow and Ringo and John and George and Paul are alive and well and full of hope. The world is still spinning and so are we and so are you. When the spinning stops—that'll be the time to worry, not before. Until then, the Beatles are alive and well and the beat goes on, the beat goes on, the beat goes on."

paul took out a lawsuit on December 31, 1970, to dissolve the Beatles' partnership, and a High Court Order placed the Beatles' affairs in the hands of a receiver. John, George, and Ringo appealed, but later dropped their appeal in the face of legal costs of over one hundred thousand pounds, on April 27, 1971.

in a *Rolling Stone* interview published in January 1971, John called Paul's solo album "rubbish," Ringo's "Good, but I wouldn't buy any of it," and said of George's, "Personally, at home, I wouldn't play that kind of music."

releases and sales

"please Please Me" was the first of fifteen consecutive number one U.K. hits for the Beatles.

please *Please Me* the album was released on March 22, 1963, and entered the U.K. charts on March 27 at the number nine slot. In seven weeks it reached number one, and remained there for twenty-nine weeks more.

despite this record-breaking success, Capitol Records in the United States passed on the album. It was instead picked up by Vee Jay Records, a small independent label, and released as *Introducing the Beatles*. The first release did not include the U.K. hit "Please Please Me" or "Ask Me Why."

emi brought in Angus McBean, a well-known theatrical and cinematic photographer, to shoot the cover for *Please Please Me*. His famous shot of the Beatles looking down from the EMI building was repeated, at the same spot and by the same photographer, for the *Let It Be* album. The shot was not used, however, until it was selected for *The Beatles 1962–1966*.

the stairwell has become something of a shrine to the Beatles. When the EMI offices relocated to Brook Green, London, in 1995, the stairwell was taken apart and reassembled at the new location.

"twist and Shout" was released as the Beatles' first EP in England in July 1963, with "A Taste of Honey," "Do You Want to Know a Secret," and "There's a Place." All of these songs were on the album *Please Please Me* as well. After one month, the EP had sold a quarter million copies, and became the first EP to enter the top ten in the British singles charts.

following *Please Please Me,* the Beatles released "From Me to You," with "Thank You Girl" as B-side, and "She Loves You" with "I'll Get You." "She Loves You" entered the charts at number two on August 28, 1963, five days after release. It took only until September 4 for the single to reach number one, a place it held for four weeks. It became a number one hit again on November 20, and held the spot for another two weeks. "She Loves You" sold 1.3 million copies in 1963, becoming Britain's best-selling single, an honor it held until 1978.

Still, Capitol Records would not release the song in the United States, and Vee Jay, which had released two other Beatles singles with little success, also let it go. It was finally released in the States on Swan. When it was rereleased in September 1963, it took until February 1, 1964 to hit the

Top Forty. It then moved to number one, held the top spot for two weeks, and remained in the *Billboard* Top Twenty for a total of fourteen weeks.

while "She Loves You" was at number one, the Beatles also took number two with "I Want to Hold Your Hand," number three with "Please Please Me," number seven with "Twist and Shout," and number fourteen with "I Saw Her Standing There."

"i Want to Hold Your Hand" was released in the United Kingdom on November 29, 1963. In a week, it began its *six-week reign* as number one in the charts. By the time the single was released in the United States, its sales in the United Kingdom had reached nearly 1.5 million. When it was displaced by "Glad All Over" by the Dave Clark Five, the *Daily Express* proclaimed it was all over for the Beatles with the headline "Tottenham Sound Has Crushed the Beatles."

only four months after the release of their first album, the Beatles started work on *With the Beatles,* recorded from July 18 to October 23, 1963. Released on November 22, 1963, the album displaced *Please Please Me* from the number one spot on the United Kingdom charts in just five days. It remained number one for twenty-one weeks, which gave the Beatles an unprecedented total of fifty continuous weeks at number one. It was the second record in history to sell a million copies in Britain.

The striking photograph of the band members on the cover was taken by Robert Freeman, who used the half-light technique of Richard Avedon. The EMI executives were all opposed to the cover, seeing it as a departure from the "happy" Beatles.

In the United States, the album was released as *Meet the Beatles* on January 20, 1964. After selling 750,000 in its first week, it went on to sell 3.65 million by the second week in March. The American version excluded the songs "Please Mr. Postman," "Roll Over Beethoven," "You Really Got a Hold on Me," "Devil in Her Heart," and "Money." However, the United States release added three songs: "I Want to Hold Your Hand," "I Saw Her Standing There," and "This Boy."

with the "I Want to Hold Your Hand" single, released in the U.S. on January 13, 1964, the Beatles finally broke the resistance of the United States Top Forty on January 25. The single quickly proceeded to number one, becoming the fastest-selling British single ever released in the States, and stayed at number one for seven weeks. It spent a total of fourteen weeks in the Top Forty.

in the United Kingdom, the *A Hard Day's Night* album went to number one in five days, and was finally taken down twenty-one weeks later by *Beatles for Sale*. In the United States, the album took from June 26, 1964, to late July to make the top spot in the charts. Once arrived, it stayed up top for fourteen weeks, selling two million copies in four months.

a four-song EP, *Extracts from the Film* A Hard Day's Night, was released on November 4, 1964. It was the first Beatles EP to miss the top thirty in Britain completely.

"can't Buy Me Love" hit the U.K. charts at number one four days after it was released on March 20, 1964. In the States, where the single sold 2.1 million copies in advance (total advance sales in the U.S. and U.K. were a record 3 million), it spent nine weeks on the *Billboard* Top Forty, five of those weeks resting at number one.

when "Can't Buy Me Love" reached number one in the States, on April 4, 1964, it joined "Twist and Shout" at number two, "She Loves You" at number three, "I Want to Hold Your Hand" at number four, and "Please Please Me" at number five. No other band had ever swept the top five like this. In the second week of "Can't Buy Me

Love" 's reign, the Beatles held fourteen singles in the Hot 100.

recording for the Beatles' fourth album began on August 11, 1964—only two months after *A Hard Day's Night* had been released—and was finished on October 26. The release of *Beatles for Sale* in December 1964 made it the fourth British Beatles album in twenty-one months.

The United States version, *Beatles '65,* featured eight songs from the U.K. version, both sides of a single, and one song from *A Hard Day's Night.* Within six weeks, the album sold three million copies, a million of those in its first week.

The album held the U.K. charts' number one spot for nine weeks after displacing *A Hard Day's Night.* The next album, *Help!,* would sell a million copies even before release.

the Beatles were outraged when they discovered that the U.S. version of *Help!* was markedly different from the U.K. version. Of the fourteen songs recorded for the album, only those seven which appeared in the film of the same name were included on the U.S. release. The second side of the album consisted of orchestral arrangements from the film's soundtrack.

the U.K. album cover of *Help!* shows the group spelling out "help" in semaphore, a signaling language which typically uses flags or lamps to signify letters. Some say that when read as a mirror-image, the Beatles spell out LPUS, or "help us."

***

the movie was originally titled *Eight Arms to Hold You,* but was changed at a late date to *Help!* The first run of the single of the title song contains the caption: "From the United Artists screenplay, *Eight Arms to Hold You.*"

***

the original Beatles' version of "Yesterday" has received more airplay than any other song ever written, with over six million plays on the radio. This is at least two million plays more than the Beatles' "Michelle," the second most-played song. Both are performed by Paul without the other band members.

***

wary of keeping their rock 'n' roll image intact, the Beatles would not permit "Yesterday" to go out as a single in the U.K. until 1976. In the U.S., however, Capitol released the "Yesterday" single in September 1965, which unsurprisingly spent nine weeks in the Top Forty, with four weeks at number one.

***

"day Tripper" was planned as an A-side single, but was pushed aside when Paul came up with "We Can Work It

Out." John, the original inspiration behind "Day Tripper," voiced his discontent, and the single was eventually released as a "double A-side." Paul and John's tributes to Liverpool, "Strawberry Fields Forever" and "Penny Lane," would also receive the double A-side treatment, but the experiment was not repeated when another of John's songs, "I Am the Walrus," lost the A-side to Paul's more commercial "Hello Goodbye."

the distorted cover photo of *Rubber Soul* was taken at John's house in Weybridge, Surrey, by Robert Freeman, who claimed that "the distorted effect in the photo was a reflection of the changing shape of [the Beatles'] lives." The photo was Robert Freeman's last cover image for the Beatles.

"rubber soul," according to Paul, referred to both the sole of shoes and soul music.

before Paul came up with "rubber soul," the intention was to call the album *The Magic Circle*.

in the U.K., *Rubber Soul* remained at number one for twelve weeks, while in the U.S., the album was at number one for six weeks and sold 1.2 million copies in its first nine days. However, none of the tracks made it to number one in the U.S. singles charts. The best-performing song on the album was "Nowhere Man," which started at number twenty-five and reached as high as number three.

after *Rubber Soul,* the Beatles released the single "Paperback Writer" on May 30, 1966. It was the first Beatles single since "She Loves You," released in August 1963, which failed to enter the chart at number one, taking a week to achieve the spot which must have by then seemed reserved exclusively for Beatles singles. The single also went to number one in Singapore, Malaysia, Australia, New Zealand, Holland, Hong Kong, Denmark, West Germany, Austria, and Ireland.

the Beatles' seventh album, *Revolver,* was released on August 5, 1966, after recording sessions that lasted from April 6 to June 21. In the United Kingdom, it enjoyed seven weeks at the top of the charts, while in the United States, it took nearly a month to reach number one and remained there for six weeks.

the United States *Revolver* lacked three songs by John: "I'm Only Sleeping," "And Your Bird Can Sing," and "Doctor Robert." All of these had been previously released on the compilation *Yesterday and Today,* which was only for the U.S. market.

yesterday *and Today* was the intended carrier of the infamous "butcher cover," which showed the Beatles dressed in white butcher coats, splattered in "blood," and holding parts of plastic dolls. It was their own idea, and at this time they were powerful enough to push it through EMI and Epstein. 750,000 sleeves were printed, and the gory image appeared on the cover of *Disc* magazine, before complaints started coming in from disk jockeys who had received advance copies. The concept was killed at a cost of two hundred thousand dollars.

John would go on to say that the cover was a comment on how the United States record companies "butchered" their early albums, both in content and packaging.

the collage on the album sleeve of *Revolver* was of a collection of photographs of the Beatles clipped by John, Paul, and longtime friend Pete Shotton. The line drawing was done by Klaus Voorman, who knew the group from their days in Hamburg. Voorman won a Grammy Award for the artwork. He later designed the *Anthology* and *Anthology II* covers.

"eleanor Rigby" was released as a single the same day *Revolver* was released, and reached the top of the U.K. singles charts on August 17. In the United States, it was in the Top

Forty for six weeks, but only reached as high as number eleven.

On the B-side to "Eleanor Rigby" was "Yellow Submarine," which fared a little better in the U.S. charts, reaching number two and spending eight weeks in the Top Forty.

In the United Kingdom, the "Strawberry Fields Forever"/"Penny Lane" single stayed at number two for two weeks before progressing to number one. During that time the number one spot was held by Engelbert Humperdinck with "Release Me." The British press marked the occasion with headlines such as "Beatles Fail to Reach the Top," and "Has the Bubble Burst?" The single was also from one of the Beatles' most unproductive periods. They had recorded only these two songs, and "When I'm Sixty-Four," in the last three months, and EMI was, for the first time, in the position of nearly begging for a release.

considered by many to be the height of the Beatles' creative collaboration, *Sgt. Pepper's Lonely Hearts Club Band* was an immediate critical and commercial success. The *New York Review of Books* claimed it was the hallmark of a "new and golden renaissance of song," while *Newsweek* compared the Beatles to T.S. Eliot: " 'A Day in the Life' is the Beatles' *Waste Land*." Released in the United Kingdom on June 1, 1967, the album sold half a million in its first month and reached the million mark in April 1973. In the United States, after advance sales in excess of one million, it broke 2.5

million copies in three months. The *Billboard* charts listed the album at number one for fifteen weeks, and it stayed in the Top 100 for over a year and a half.

the famous cover of *Sgt. Pepper* represented the Beatles as a small-town ensemble, with a crowd behind them. The faces for the crowd were picked by the Beatles, and Brian Epstein's personal assistant, Wendy Moger, put in "many hours" to gain permission from those (still living) whose photographs would be on the cover. Shirley Temple would only agree if she could hear the record first. Mae West refused at first, but agreed to have her picture on the cover after the Beatles all wrote her individually. The only refusal was from Leo Gorcey, who wanted to be paid. The figures were assembled into a three-dimensional collage, with the other cover elements in the foreground.

Among those intended for the cover but who neglected to give permission or were removed were Brigitte Bardot, Adolf Hitler, René Magritte, and Alfred Jarry. Mahatma Gandhi was intended for the cover, but EMI, which did quite a bit of business in India, thought it would be taken as an insult to have this holy man on a rock album. He was removed.

The cover was designed by British artist Peter Blake, who was a successful painter represented by the Robert Fraser Gallery (which would later exhibit John and Yoko). He was paid two hundred pounds for the cover. In 1983, Blake's retrospective at the Tate Gallery in London became the most successful show ever held at London's most prominent contemporary art gallery.

EMI, which usually spent from twenty-five to seventy-five pounds on photography for album sleeves, received a bill for over £1,300 for permissions and processing, plus another

£1,500 in fees for the artist, Peter Blake, and the consultants, Robert Fraser and Michael Cooper.

The time and money spent on the album's songs were similarly lavish: over seven hundred hours in the studio and $75,000. Every sound recorded in the studio, vocal and instrumental, went through some sort of technological distortion.

Sgt. *Pepper* was perhaps the first record package which contained a printed inside sleeve, a design done by the Dutch design group The Fool. The colored sleeve only appears on packages from the first pressings. *Sgt. Pepper* is also proclaimed to be the first popular album which printed a complete set of lyrics.

the original album contains a high-frequency note in the run-out groove of side two, audible to dogs but not to the human listeners of the album. It also contains two seconds cut from the Beatles singing the first thing that came to their minds when George Martin started recording and cut into tape loops. Martin resurrected this experiment for the CD version of the album, with several revolutions which then fade to silence.

paul was the main inspiration and drive behind the "concept" of the album—the Beatles masquerading as a band tied to a fictional Sgt. Pepper. John, however, was more skeptical, and in his 1980 *Playboy* interview openly derided the idea: "It doesn't go anywhere. All my contributions to the album have absolutely nothing to do with this idea of Sgt. Pepper and his band; but it works 'cause we *said* it worked."

the *Magical Mystery Tour* album, released on December 8, 1967, in the United Kingdom, was a soundtrack to the movie of the same name conceived by McCartney. The U.K. package consisted of the six soundtrack songs on two EPS, and never reached higher than number two on the singles charts, with the "Hello Goodbye" single keeping it from number one. The United States version included, in addition to the soundtrack, the singles released in 1967, and sold 50,000 copies as an import to the United Kingdom—the biggest-selling import in U.K. recording history—before it was officially released by EMI as a UK album in 1976. Two songs appeared in the film which were on neither the U.K. or U.S. albums— "Shirley's Wild Accordion" and "Jessie's Dream."

"hey Jude" was released as a single, with "Revolution" on the B-side, simultaneously in the United Kingdom and United States on August 26, 1968. It quickly went to number one in both countries, and also topped the charts in Ireland, New Zealand, Holland, West Germany, Belgium, Singapore, Malaysia, Denmark, Norway, and Sweden. It went on to become the Beatles' best-selling single, reaching five million in sales by late 1968, and seven and a half million by late

1972. In 1976, *Billboard* listed "Hey Jude" as the second best-selling single of the previous twenty years.

the "Hey Jude"/"Revolution" single was the first record released by the Beatles' own Apple Records, a division of Apple Corps.

yellow *Submarine,* released in January 1969, featured only four new songs: "Only a Northern Song," "All Together Now," "Hey Bulldog," and "It's All Too Much." It was filled out with a few previously released Beatles singles and orchestrations by George Martin. It only reached number three on the U.K. charts, while the White Album was at number one. In the United States, it entered the Top 100 at 86, and eventually made it to number two, where it stayed for a week.

known as "the White Album" for its plain white cover, *The Beatles* was the first Beatles album released on the Apple label, and quickly became the best-selling double album ever seen. In the United States, it sold four million copies in one month, and wasn't beaten by another double album until 1977, when it was topped by the *Saturday Night Fever* soundtrack.

the cover and insert were done by Richard Hamilton, who had been well-known in London since the late 1950s for his pop art. The early pressings are numbered, as if for a limited edition. John, who moved most quickly, got *The Beatles* number 00001.

as several critics have commented, the arrangement of *Abbey Road* reflects the rifts coming between John and Paul late in the Beatles' history. John had wanted a stronger rock 'n' roll sound, while Paul was tending toward a pop orchestra album, with all the songs running together. In the end, the second side of the album ran the songs together, while the first presented them individually.

in an *Evening Standard* interview after the Beatles had broken up, Paul expressed regret about the politics between band members that influenced their music. As an example, he spoke of how he would have liked to sing harmony on John's "Come Together": ". . . but I was too embarrassed to ask him and I don't work to the best of my abilities in that situation."

paul admitted that he was being overbearing as he attempted to fill the role of a producer during the *Abbey Road* sessions. George Martin claims that the group was splintering in other ways as well, with each member bringing in his own musicians for the songs he had written. However, the album was finished in less than a month, more quickly than any since the Beatles first started recording.

abbey *Road* went straight to number one in the U.S. and Britain, and went on to become the best-selling Beatles album, with sales of over ten million in its first ten years.

although *Let It Be* was the last Beatles album to be released, on May 8, 1970, after the group broke up, it was recorded during the making of the film by the same name, several months before recording started for *Abbey Road*.

The album was released in the U.K. as a box set with a book called *The Beatles Get Back*. The sleeve of the album proclaimed that it marked a "new phase" in their music, which looked ridiculous, since the band had already dissolved.

the advance orders for *Let It Be* in the United States were 3.7 million, breaking all previous records for advance orders, including those recently set by the Beatles themselves.

all of the Beatles' songs released during their reign over the music charts add up to only ten and one-half hours of music. They left a legacy of over four hundred hours of tape in Abbey Road's archives.

song inspiration and composition

the Beatles were, in the beginning, typically only given two weeks' notice to prepare for a recording session. Later, they could call their own studio times, and frequently came in unrehearsed.

they rarely wore headphones in the studio.

two versions of "Love Me Do" were released. The first was recorded September 4, 1962, featured Ringo on drums, and was released as a single. Later pressings would use version two. The second version, released on the album, was demanded by George Martin, who wasn't satisfied with Ringo's drumming after seventeen takes and replaced him with session musician Andy White. Ringo played tambourine on the second version.

on "Love Me Do," John plays a harmonica, which he said he shoplifted from a store in Holland.

the suggestion to include the harmonica came from George Martin, who asked for a "bluesy thing." Until John was required to fill in with the harmonica, the conclusion of the chorus was his to sing. It now passed to Paul.

---

john wrote "Please Please Me" in imitation of Roy Orbison, and picked up on Bing Crosby's play on "please" and "pleas" in the first line of "Please."

---

a slow version of the song was recorded on September 11, 1962, but was never released. George Martin brought them back into the studio for a more up-tempo take.

---

when they finished the final take of "Please Please Me," George Martin announced to them over the intercom, "Gentlemen, you've just made your first number one record."

---

the Beatles' first four releases all have the words "me" or "you" in the title. Paul claimed this was a commercial choice, to make the band more "personal": "A lot of our songs were directly addressed to our fans. Personal pronouns. We always used to do that."

the last verse of "Please Please Me" has John and Paul accidentally singing different lyrics on one line.

"ask Me Why" appeared on the B-side of "Please Please Me," as well as the album. It also appeared on the *All My Loving* EP, released in February 1964.

while the credit for the Beatles' first single reads Lennon/McCartney, the two follow-up singles and the *Please Please Me* album credit McCartney/Lennon. The issue was finally resolved by their musical publishing company, which dictated Lennon/McCartney. Paul complained about this in his authorized biography: " 'Why Lennon and McCartney? Why not McCartney and Lennon?' 'It sounds better,' they said. 'Not to me it doesn't,' I said."

the surprising success of the "Please Please Me" single led to a rushed release of the *Please Please Me* album, recorded in one session (except for those songs already recorded as singles) at Abbey Road Studios on February 11, 1963. Sources disagree on how long it took to record the album, but it seems to have taken anywhere from 9¾ hours to 16 hours. Abbey Road archivist Mark Lewisohn called it the most productive 585 minutes in the history of recorded music.

recording costs for *Please Please Me* added up to a mere four hundred pounds. The band was rushed to finish the album, due to a demand for live performances, and John was coming down with a cold. A bowl of cough drops was placed on the piano, next to a carton of cigarettes.

"twist and Shout" was a favorite during the Beatles' live performances, but John's vocal interpretation consisted of screaming the lyrics, as Martin remarked: "God alone knows what he did to his larynx each time he performed it, because he made a sound like tearing flesh." Martin, considering John's already sore throat, said of the recording session: "That *had* to be right on the first take, because I knew perfectly well that if we had to do it a second time it would never be as good." John, according to a recording engineer at the session, "stripped to the waist to do the most amazingly raucous vocal." The band did the song in one take.

"i Saw Her Standing There" was another early collaboration between Paul and John, written in Paul's living room in September 1962.

paul admitted that he directly copied the bass line of "I Saw Her Standing There" from "I'm Talking About You" by Chuck Berry.

songs the Beatles covered on *Please Please Me* included "Chains," originally recorded by the Cookies; "Boys" and "Baby It's You," recorded by the Shirelles; "A Taste of Honey," written by Ric Marlow and Bobby Scott for the play *A Taste of Honey*; and "Twist and Shout," originally recorded by the Isley Brothers.

paul and John saw "From Me to You" as a major breakthrough in their growth as composers. In the middle eight section, instead of going the familiar rock 'n' roll route of C to A minor, they experimented with C to G minor. Paul recalled, "That middle eight was a very big departure for us. Going to G minor and a C takes you to a whole new world. It was exciting."

john took as a starting point for "Do You Want to Know a Secret" a song his mother sang for him: "Wishing Well" from Walt Disney's *Snow White*.

"all My Loving" was for John a favorite among Paul's compositions. In an interview, he praised it by saying that he wished he had written it himself. Paul wrote the song while on a tour bus, and says that it was the first time in his songwriting career that he had finished the lyrics before he started on the music.

"i Want to Hold Your Hand" was written by Paul and John in Jane Asher's house on the piano. The song was recorded on October 17, 1963, at Abbey Road, and marked the first song for which the Beatles used four-track recording equipment. The B-side, "This Boy," was recorded the same day. Prior to this song, the Beatles only had two-track recording available to them, which meant that each member had to perform his part perfectly at the same time, as the option of overdubs was not available.

the Beatles recorded a German version of "I Want to Hold Your Hand"—"Komm, Gib Mir Deine Hand"—at the insistence of EMI Germany. The recording can be found on *Rarities* in the U.K., *Something New* in the U.S., and on *Past Masters, Volume 1.*

ringo was generally credited for coining the phrase "a hard day's night" while on the set of the still untitled movie. Ringo was particularly worn down from the grueling schedule of recording the album while shooting the film, not to mention putting in several live performances and radio appearances. On June 3, 1964, Ringo collapsed from exhaustion and missed performances in Northern Europe, Hong Kong, and Australia. He was released from the hospital on June 11.

Credit might also go to John, who had coincidentally included the phrase "Hard Day's Night" in the short story "Sad Michael," which appeared in *In His Own Write,* published earlier that year. John wrote the song overnight after it was suggested that the film be titled after Ringo's comment.

John was at this point at the peak of his creative output. On the *A Hard Day's Night* album, ten of the thirteen songs were written primarily by him.

Recording "A Hard Day's Night" commenced immediately the next day, so the writing, rehearsing, and recording were all finished in roughly twenty-four hours.

George Harrison plays a twelve-string guitar on this song, which was a new addition to his growing collection of instruments, and Ringo plays bongos in addition to drums.

George's twelve-string provides the two-second opening chord that has fascinated musicians and commentators alike. The chord has been variously described as a dominant ninth of F, a G7 with added ninth and suspended fourth, and a G eleventh suspended fourth. The song closes with a fade that has George picking the individual notes of the chord. The effects are subtle, but caused George Martin to realize that his charges had moved on to another level.

paul wrote "Can't Buy Me Love" with some help from John, while the two were staying in Paris for an engagement at the Olympia Theater. George Martin came to Paris so they could record the song for the *A Hard Day's Night* soundtrack at the Pathé Marconi Studios. Paul laid down the final vocal track almost one month later in London.

Paul objected strongly to the suggestion that "Can't Buy Me Love" was referring to prostitution: "Personally, I think you can put any interpretation you want to anything, but when someone says 'Can't Buy Me Love' is about prostitution, I draw the line. That's going too far.''

in contrast to *A Hard Day's Night*, which featured all-original material, *Beatles for Sale*'s fourteen tracks consisted of only eight originals.

the feedback in the opening of "I Feel Fine" was brought into the song after John leaned his guitar against an amp and produced an unexpected high whine. Paul called it a musical "found object," and it is often cited as the first Beatle acoustic experiment, although the same has been said of the mixing on the fade-out of "What You're Doing," for which they altered their instruments' sound by overriding or "defeating" the mixing desk.

John boasted of this discovery as the first instance of controlled feedback on record: "I defy anybody to find a record—unless it's some old blues record in 1922—that uses feedback that way." On a separate occasion, he said, "I claim it for the Beatles. Before Hendrix, before the Who, before anybody. The first feedback on record." However, he later acknowledged that many of his contemporaries were using feedback live.

paul picked up the title for "Eight Days a Week" from an overheard comment, but has given two different sources for his inspiration. In his 1984 *Playboy* interview, he said it, like "A Hard Day's Night," was based on a comment by Ringo on how tired he was: "He said it as though he were an overworked chauffeur." However, in his 1997 authorized biography, he attributed the comment to an actual chauffeur, one of John's.

The very first pop song to open with a fade-*in* was "Eight Days a Week." The fade-in was made even more effective as the opening to the second side of the album *Beatles for Sale*.

"she's a Woman" may contain the Beatles' first reference to drugs, with the use of the slang phrase for getting someone high, "turn me on."

"baby's in Black" was an unusual composition for Paul and John, being written in ¾ time. They would announce it in their performances as "something different."

paul wrote "I'll Follow the Sun" when he was just sixteen, and was never quite pleased with the composition. It was apparently included on *Beatles for Sale* due to lack of other new material.

their next album sessions, for *Help!*, produced two Lennon/McCartney songs which didn't make the album, and are still secure in the Abbey Road vault; Ringo singing "If You've Got Trouble," and "That Means a Lot." One commentator, Mark Hertsgaard, who heard the songs, claimed that they are not by any means "undiscovered Beatles masterpieces." The former was dropped after one take, while the latter needed twenty-four takes before being rejected.

john originally wrote "Help!" as a much slower, reflective song. This was, however, not seen as a commercially viable tempo for the title track of an album and a movie. John would later speak derisively about the decision to speed up the song.

for "You've Got to Hide Your Love Away," the Beatles brought in studio musicians, for the first time since Ringo was replaced on drums for the Beatles' first single, to add flutes to the arrangement.

"ticket to Ride" had a double meaning, as Ryde, in the Isle of Wight, was where Paul's cousin and her husband lived. The fade-out at the end of the song was an innovation for Paul and John, since they faded out while singing new lyrics, instead of going back to the first verse, which most of their songs did.

Lennon called "Ticket to Ride" "one of the earliest heavy-metal records made."

one of Paul's favorite compositions is "I've Just Seen a Face," which he mostly wrote himself. His later band, Wings, would include this and only a few other Beatle songs in their repertoire.

"yesterday " also marked a turning point for the group, being the first song recorded by only one member of the group, Paul, alone with studio musicians on violins. It was also the first to get airplay on adult-oriented radio stations in the United States.

The strings on "Yesterday" were originally George Martin's idea.

Paul woke up one day with the basic tune for "Yesterday" playing in his head, and spent longer working out the lyrics than he ever had on any song before. He was at first convinced that it was not his—that he had heard the tune somewhere and simply forgot the source. "I couldn't believe it. It came too easy," he remarked.

john had a similar experience of inexplicable inspiration with "Nowhere Man": "I'd spent five hours that morning trying to write a song that was meaningful and good, and I finally gave up and lay down. Then 'Nowhere Man' came, words and music, the whole damn thing, as I lay down."

"act Naturally" gave Ringo a chance to sing, and was given the B-side to the "Yesterday" single in the States. The Buck

Owens version of this Johnny Russell and Voni Morrison song was a hit in 1963. Ringo performed the song on the 1965 British and American tours, *The Ed Sullivan Show,* the *Cilla* show in 1965, and the *Ringo* TV special in 1978. He recorded another version at Abbey Road in 1989, with Buck Owens himself.

the *Help!* album marked another development for the Beatles, in their use of new instruments and studio musicians. Besides the studio musicians on "Yesterday" and "You've Got to Hide Your Love Away," Lennon was recorded playing an electric piano for the first time and Harrison played his composition "I Need You" on a tone pedal guitar, another first. Paul and George Martin played together on a Steinway piano on "You Like Me Too Much."

"we Can Work It Out" was very much a group effort, although Paul was responsible for most of it. John wrote the middle eight ("Life is very short . . ."), and George suggested that the middle eight be done in ¾ time. They also put to use an aging harmonium they found in the studio.

the Beatles would also use the harmonium on "The Word" and "If I Needed Someone."

the songs for *Rubber Soul,* excluding "Wait," which was recorded originally for *Help!,* were written and recorded in less than four weeks. The final group session for *Rubber Soul* lasted thirteen solid hours.

with *Rubber Soul,* the Beatles moved from writing songs to working on albums. "We had been making albums rather like a collection of singles," remarked George Martin. "Now we were really beginning to think about albums as a bit of art on their own."

"norwegian Wood" has been widely proclaimed to be the first pop song to use a sitar. Harrison picked up a "crummy" sitar in London after hearing one on the set of the movie *Help!* and tuned it to Western notes for "Norwegian Wood." The sitar was dubbed in later, as it took some time for Harrison, still learning how to play the instrument, to get the part right.

Paul says the title for "Norwegian Wood" came from a small decorating craze in London, when everyone was having their rooms redone in wood from Norway.

"the Word" was written collaboratively by John and Paul. After they finished, they got high and colored their lyric sheet with crayons. This manuscript was later given by John to John Cage for his collection of manuscript scores, and turned up in *Notations,* a selection from Cage's collection.

"what Goes On" was the first song for which Ringo received a songwriting credit, but he told an interviewer that his contribution amounted to "about five words." He and Paul contributed to Lennon's original lyrics while they were in the studio. Ringo also sings lead vocal.

john convinced Paul to do "Michelle" based on Paul's joking performance of bad French at parties. For the lyrics, he had Ivan Vaughan's wife, Jan, who was a French teacher, give him rhymes and translations. He later sent her a check for her contribution.

while arranging "Girl" in the studio, the Beatles got a big laugh out of working "tit tit tit tit" into the song, making it sound just enough like "dit dit dit dit" to get away with it. John also can be heard taking a long lingering breath of air, which to many sound like an inhalation off a joint.

lennon called "In My Life" his first "real major piece of work . . . the first time I consciously put [the] literary part

177

of myself into the lyric." Paul recalls writing the music for the song, but John remembered things differently. George Martin himself played the piano part that he composed for the middle eight, a part he added, while the Beatles were out of the studio, to fulfill John's vague instructions for "something baroque-sounding." Martin recorded his part at half-speed and then played it back at twice the normal speed to achieve a harpsichord-like sound.

the original lyrics that Paul had fitted into the tune of "Drive My Car" were along the lines of "I can give you diamond rings/I can give you anything/Baby I love you." John called these lyrics "crap," which Paul already knew: " 'Rings' is fatal anyway, 'rings' always rhymes with 'things' and I knew it was a bad idea." Keeping the tune intact, the two songwriters contrived a story about an ambitious woman, complete with the sexual overtones taken from blues songs about driving and chauffeurs.

according to those who have heard the unreleased takes of "I'm Looking Through You," the earlier versions, in particular the first take, are much softer, or in the words of writer Mark Hertsgaard, who gained access to the tapes, "less of an attack and more of a disappointed revelation." The Beatles archivist at Abbey Road, Mark Lewisohn, said that the first take was the best alternate take in the 400-plus hours of recorded material at Abbey Road.

the B-side to "Paperback Writer" was "Rain," the first Beatles song to use backward tape loops. John came up with the idea when he was listening to a preliminary recording "stoned out of my mind." The fade-out is John singing the opening lines backwards. "Rain" achieved its heavy sound through the band's playing faster than usual, and then slowing the tape down to alter the frequency of their instruments.

ringo has said that his best performance on record is on "Rain." "I think it was the first time I used this trick of starting a break by hitting the hi-hat first instead of going directly to a drum off the hi-hat."

the authorship of "Eleanor Rigby" has been hotly disputed; it's credited to both John and Paul, as were all their other songs. John claimed he wrote about "seventy percent" of the song, while Paul contests he wrote "about half a line." Pete Shotton attributes the song to Paul.

According to Paul, "Eleanor Rigby" received its name from a store called "Rigby," and the actress Eleanor Bron who worked with the Beatles on the movie *Help!* The other character in the song, father MacKenzie, was picked at random from a phone book. Paul originally thought of calling the character "Father McCartney," but worried about placing his father in a "lonely song."

Paul has been told that there is a gravestone marked "Eleanor Rigby" in Woolton, Liverpool, where John and Paul used to spend time as teenagers. However, he denies that this was a conscious inspiration.

ON "Yellow Submarine," the studio "effects" included bubbles blown into tanks, chains being shaken, and Paul and John speaking into small hand mikes to produce the sound of the "crew."

"love You To," another George Harrison composition, was the first song he wrote specifically for the sitar. As he remarked in his autobiography, " 'Norwegian Wood' was an accident as far as the sitar was concerned."

"here, There and Everywhere," written by Paul as he sat next to John's pool, was one of John's very favorite Beatles songs.

"she Said She Said" was written by John after an acid trip he took in Los Angeles with the members of the Byrds. He said in an interview: "Peter Fonda came in when we were on acid and he kept coming up to me and sitting next to me and whispering, 'I know what it's like to be dead.' He was describing an acid trip he'd been on."

another drug-influenced Lennon song on *Revolver* was "Doctor Robert." Paul and Pete Shotton claimed that the song was about a New York doctor who gave generous prescriptions, but Lennon said that the song was about himself: "I was the one that carried all the pills on tour . . . in the early days."

also heavily influenced by psychedelics, but with a good measure of Tibetan spirituality, was Lennon's "Tomorrow Never Knows." Lennon had been tripping heavily and reading Timothy Leary and Richard Alpert's *The Psychedelic Experience,* as well as the Tibetan *Book of the Dead*. In the studio, he wanted his voice to sound like a lama singing on a hilltop, and Martin used a rotating speaker to create the effect. Paul said he mixed a series of tape loops for the song, using five machines and five assistants to keep or give tension as directed. Paul claimed that the words were from the Tibetan *Book of the Dead*.

george Martin called the tape loop a "primitive synthesizer," and explained how "the mix became a performance" in a conversation with Beatles insider John Burgess: "While mixing, whatever you brought up at the time would be there. We wouldn't know what point of the loop would appear. It was a random thing. So 'Tomorrow Never Knows' can never be remixed again, because all those things happened at that time in that particular way. It's one of the greatest things about that record. It is a page in history that happened there, can't happen again."

"**got** to Get You into My Life," recorded on April 7 and 8, 1966, marked the first time the Beatles used a brass section on one of their songs.

Paul remarked that this song is about nothing else but marijuana: "It's not to a person, it's actually about pot. It's saying, 'I'm going to do this. This is not a bad idea.' So it's actually an ode to pot, like someone else might write an ode to chocolate or a good claret."

"**fixing** a Hole," which appears on *Sgt. Pepper's Lonely Hearts Club Band,* was another ode to pot, according to Paul, although many took it to be an ode to heroin and the need for a "fix."

"**penny** Lane" and "Strawberry Fields Forever" were intended for an album of songs about the Beatles' childhood memories of Liverpool, but were released as a single when Capitol demanded a new release. The concept of the childhood album was shelved.

The high brass sound on "Penny Lane" comes from a piccolo trumpet, which plays an octave above a normal trumpet. McCartney heard the trumpet at a performance of Bach's *Brandenburg Concerti.*

While working on "Penny Lane" Paul worked in a few inside jokes, including the line about "finger pie," a reference to females, intended for "the Liverpool lads who like a bit of smut."

John wrote "Strawberry Fields Forever" while he was filming *How I Won the War*, in Almería, Spain. "Strawberry Fields" is a reference not to a piece of natural Liverpool scenery, but to a Salvation Army home in Liverpool where John attended parties as a child.

The Beatles first recorded the song with just the four of them on their usual instruments, but later John wanted more orchestration—harpsichord, tympani, trumpet, cellos, horns. The second version appealed to John, but he liked the beginning of the first version. George Martin combined the two versions, despite the fact that they were in different tempos and keys, by slowing down one version and speeding up the other.

John called this song one of his only "honest" songs. The other is "Help!"

the Beatles played a vast range of instruments for *Sgt. Pepper,* according to their fan newsletter, including "fourteen guitars, a tamboura, one sitar, a two-manual Vox organ, and Ringo's Ludwig kit. Plus various pianos and organs supplied by EMI."

The band also made use of the EMI sound library. The laughter from the audience in the title track was from an actual performance by Dudley Moore, Peter Cook, Alan Bennett, and Jonathan Miller called *Beyond the Fringe*. Including the laughter was a private joke that Paul couldn't resist based on his days listening to radio shows. As he told his biographer Barry Miles: "There would always be a moment in these things, because it was live radio, where [the MC] wouldn't say anything, and the audience would laugh. And my imagination went wild when that happened. I thought, What is it? Has he dropped his trousers?"

according to the Beatles and witnesses, and contrary to the conventional interpretation, "Lucy in the Sky with Diamonds" was not written with the LSD acronym in mind. John was inspired to write the song after seeing a drawing by his son Julian of one of his schoolmates, Lucy, in a diamond-studded sky. The drawing was titled *Lucy in the Sky with Diamonds*. John and Paul claimed the imagery in the song is straight out of *Alice in Wonderland*.

"getting Better" is perhaps one of the more classic Lennon/McCartney collaborations, with Paul conceiving the very optimistic song, and John contributing the sardonic line about how it couldn't get worse, as well as the lines about being cruel to his woman.

George Harrison plays tamboura, a large Indian lute with four strings, on "Getting Better." George Martin contributed by playing piano, hitting the strings directly instead of the keys.

"she's Leaving Home," written by Paul after seeing a *Daily Mirror* article on a runaway girl from a wealthy home, featured John and Paul both on lead and backing vocal, and sessions musicians on strings and harp. No Beatles played instruments for this song. The song is also unusual in that George Martin did not arrange it. Paul called him, but couldn't get studio time, and went ahead to another source to have it arranged.

lennon wrote the lyrics to "Being for the Benefit of Mr. Kite!" almost word-for-word from a Victorian poster advertising a variety show.

John wanted a steam organ to play in the background, but of course, there were few working steam organs in London at the time. George Martin instead cut a tape of Victorian steam organs playing marches and waltzes into sections and rearranged them randomly: "When I listened to them, they formed a chaotic mass of sound. . . . It was unmistakably a steam organ."

paul says he composed the tune for "When I'm Sixty-Four" on his father's piano when he was just sixteen.

george Harrison's song "Within You Without You" features Harrison on tamboura and vocal, and musicians from the Indian Music Association on dilruba, tamboura, tabla, and swordmandel. Sessions musicians play violins and cellos, but Harrison is the only Beatle on the track.

George can be heard laughing at the end of the track. George Martin claimed that this was Harrison trying to relieve his tension and self-consciousness about his composition.

paul recalls coming up with the lyrics for "Lovely Rita" after hearing the exclusively American phrase "meter maid." However, a traffic warden named Meta claimed that she gave Paul a parking ticket on one occasion. Paul approached her as she was writing the ticket, found her name, and said it would be lovely in a song.

"good Morning, Good Morning" was inspired by a cornflakes advertisement which John heard on television. John asked for barnyard animals, which were taken from the EMI sound-effects library. John asked for the animal sounds at the end to be arranged along the lines of a food chain, with each animal growing larger or meaner than the one before it. George Martin discovered that the chicken sounds were similar to the beginning guitar on the next track, the reprise of "Sgt. Pepper," and mixed the sounds so that one turned into the other. He reminisced, "That was one of the luckiest edits one could ever get."

"a Day in the Life" remains one of the most complicated and innovative pop songs ever recorded. Lyrics were initiated by John, with Paul contributing the middle section and the line "I'd love to turn you on." Gaps in the lyrics were filled by suggestions from friends and studio engineers. The orchestra which was brought in—both John and Paul would later take credit for the inspiration behind putting an orchestra in the song, but George Martin recalls it as John's idea—was instructed to go from the lowest note on their instrument to their highest note, but were told they could decide independently how to go about it. The mostly middle-aged orchestra were all given novelty items to wear during the session, such as rubber noses, gorilla paws, or paper marks, to create a spontaneous mood. Lennon's request that the orchestra sound like "the end of the world" was thus achieved. The final chord cluster at the very end of the song was achieved by all the Beatles and George Martin on pianos, all hitting the same chord as hard as they could. As the noise died, faders were pushed up to sustain the sound. The sound level was so high by the end of the chord that, if one listens carefully, the Abbey Road air conditioning system can be heard.

Mark Lewishon, the EMI archivist who went through the massive collection of recordings for the official history of the sessions, claimed that one of John's quirks was to come up with some rhythmic nonsense rather than lead into a song with the conventional "1-2-3-4." For instance, on the "A Day in the Life" tapes," he leads in by saying "Sugarplum fairy, sugarplum fairy."

Since EMI didn't have synching machines, Martin was forced to do the synching for their overdubs by hand, a process he called "hit and miss." On "A Day in the Life," he said, "You can hear the ragged ensemble of the orchestra because there are several orchestras coming in slightly at a distance from each other."

Leonard Bernstein, in 1990, said of this song and the Lennon/McCartney partnership: "Three bars of 'A Day in the Life' will sustain me, rejuvenate me, inflame my senses and sensibilities. They are the best songwriters since Gershwin."

"**all** You Need Is Love" was written by Lennon for the live appearance of the Beatles on *Our World,* the first live worldwide broadcast. The program was six hours long and watched by an estimated 400 million people. The idea was to allow viewers to watch the Beatles recording their new single, but the recording was actually done in three parts. A backing track of harpsichord (John), string bass (Paul), violin (Harrison, playing violin for the first time), and drums (Ringo) was taped at Olympic Studios, London. Another track with the conventional guitar, bass, and drums was recorded at Abbey Road, alone with studio musicians on trumpet, trombone, saxophone, accordion, violin, and cello. These tracks were played during the live performance with a studio orchestra and a chorus which included Mick Jagger, Gary Leeds, Keith Richards, Marianne Faithfull, Jane Asher, Patti Harrison, Keith Moon, and Graham Nash.

The "All You Need Is Love" single went from composition to release more quickly than any other Beatles single. It was written at the end of May and released on July 7, 1967, with "Baby You're a Rich Man" as the B-side.

"**baby** You're a Rich Man" was recorded and mixed at Olympia Studios, London, making it the first Beatles song to be produced outside of Abbey Road Studios. The Beatles came to Olympia through the Rolling Stones, who regularly used the studio. Brian Jones, lead guitarist for the Stones, played oboe, and Mick Jagger may have provided backing vocals. John and Paul both play piano.

"flying," an instrumental that appears on the *Magical Mystery Tour* album, was the first song credited to all four Beatles. It was also the only instrumental they ever recorded for EMI.

on "I Am the Walrus," Lennon took the notes of a police siren as the basic rhythm and the title from Lewis Carroll's "The Walrus and the Carpenter."

some claim that "the eggman" was a reference to a London swinger and friend of John's who broke raw eggs over his partners during sex.

paul came up with "Hey Jude" to lift the spirits of John's son Julian while John and Cynthia were going through their breakup. He originally was singing "Hey Jules" to himself, but thought that "Jude" sounded "a bit more country and western."

At seven minutes, eleven seconds, "Hey Jude" is the longest Beatles single. The fade-out lasts approximately four minutes.

John told an interviewer that "Hey Jude" is Paul's best song, and also believes that it was a message to him. He takes "go out and get her" as a directive to establish his relationship with Yoko Ono.

the album version of "Revolution" differs from the single version in several respects. George Harrison and Paul were dissatisfied with the slower version recorded first, and asked for a faster version, which appears on the single. The album version is the slower version, and includes a brass section and McCartney on piano.

the single version also differs from the album version in the lyric about whether John should be counted 'in' or 'out' of violent acts. On the album, Lennon sings "out," then "in." He said he couldn't decide how he felt about violence, and later said it was a "yin-yang thing."

by some accounts, "Only a Northern Song" was written when the producer for *Yellow Submarine* demanded another song for the film. Harrison took the assignment and finished it in about an hour. Another source holds that it was recorded during the *Sgt. Pepper* sessions, and wasn't deemed ready for release until a song was demanded.

"all Together Now" was written by Paul, and recalls an old chant of football fans.

"hey Bulldog" was originally titled "Hey Bullfrog," but John changed the title after Paul started barking during the recording session to make John laugh. The session for "Hey Bulldog" was the first with Yoko in attendance.

"you Know My Name (Look Up the Number)," which appears on the B–side of "Let It Be," came to be through the Beatles basically playing around in the studio. The band recorded twenty minutes' worth of versions, adding to whatever they already had whenever they were in a silly mood. The versions were later edited down to fit on a single and released as something of a novelty/comedy song. Brian Jones, of the Rolling Stones, plays sax on one of the song's segments, and Mal Evans, a friend of the Beatles, shovels gravel rhythmically during another segment.

Paul named this song as "probably" his favorite Beatles track and one of his fondest memories of recording.

while writing "Lady Madonna," Paul wrote a line for each day of the week except Saturday, which he says was unintentional and he didn't discover it until 1994: "I did every other day of the week, but I missed out Saturday. So I figured it must have been a real night out."

for the White Album, the Beatles spent five months in the studio working on thirty-three songs, thirty of which went out on the album. As they approached the end of the

White Album sessions, impending deadlines required them to sometimes work in two studios at the same time. Three songs that came out of these sessions—"What's the New Mary Jane" by John, "Not Guilty" by George, and "Jubilee" by Paul—were not released on any Beatles album.

"Not Guilty" went up to 101 takes over two days before it was dropped. This was the first time the Beatles had attempted over one hundred takes. George later put it on his 1979 solo album.

"What's the New Mary Jane" was an experiment of John's where he played seemingly random notes on the piano and was backed up only by George.

"**back** in the U.S.S.R." was recorded without Ringo on drums, as he had walked out on the band during the recording session. Paul filled in on drums, as he would for "Dear Prudence." The song was a spoof of the Beach Boys and of Chuck Berry's "Back in the U.S.A." Mike Love of the Beach Boys, who was at the Maharishi's ashram as well, said he recommended the references to Georgian and Ukrainian girls.

"**dear** Prudence" was evidently inspired by Prudence Farrow, Mia Farrow's sister, who was at the Rishikesh ashram with the Beatles. She allegedly spent so much time in meditation that she rarely was seen outside of her cottage, and John was asked to speak to her about coming out to join the others. He sang the song outside the door of her hut, and she began to relax and open up.

"glass Onion," written by John with help from Paul, was done as a joke on those who took extremely serious messages out of Beatles songs. It contains references to five Beatles songs: "Strawberry Fields Forever," "I Am the Walrus," "Lady Madonna," "The Fool on the Hill," and "Fixing a Hole."

according to Alistair Taylor of NEMS, shortly after the release of the White Album, Paul received a phone call on behalf of a musician whose reggae band was named "Ob-la-di, Ob-la-da." The musician was in Brixton Prison, London, for failure to keep up with alimony payments. He asked for 111 pounds, eighteen shillings, the amount he needed to clear up the payments and be released from prison, and in return he would drop all claims to the title. Paul didn't recall seeing this band's posters or hearing of them at all, but thought he could help, and had the money delivered to Brixton Prison. McCartney's version, as told to *Playboy,* had the musician as "just one of those guys who had great expressions," who hung around the clubs and used to say "Ob-la-di, ob-la-da, life goes on." Paul also told his biographer that he sent him a check for the inspiration without being asked.

"Ob-La-Di, Ob-La-Da" was recorded three times, and finally, when John and George were convinced they had it right, Paul informed them that he had screwed up a lyric, singing "Desmond stays at home and does his pretty face," when he meant to sing "Molly." The others didn't believe him until the tape was played back. Paul settled for the version, however, and the confusion he thought it would create.

john wrote "The Continuing Story of Bungalow Bill" after meeting a participant in the Maharishi's ashram who, in John's words, "took a short break to go shoot a few poor tigers, and then came back to commune with God." Yoko Ono contributed one sung line to the song, "not when he looked so fierce," and Maureen Starkey contributed to the chorus. This was Yoko's first appearance on a record, and the first female voice on a Beatles record that was other than back-up.

george Harrison had been reading about the *I Ching,* and was fascinated with the idea of introducing random elements into his songwriting. He decided to write a song around the first thing he saw when he opened a book, picked at random from his parents' shelves. What he saw was the phrase "gently weeps," and immediately started to write "While My Guitar Gently Weeps."

The song features Eric Clapton on guitar. George Harrison thought Clapton's playing was great, but ran his part through an automatic double-tracker machine to make it wobble. He thought this made it sound more "Beatley."

a well-known fact about "Happiness Is a Warm Gun" is that John saw the caption on an American firearms magazine, shortly after the assassination of Robert F. Kennedy, which read "Happiness is a warm gun in your hand." John later remarked, "I thought, 'What a fantastic, insane thing to say.' A warm gun means that you've just shot something."

adding to the mix of different styles in the song, the drumming is in 4/4 time while the guitars are in 3/4 time. George, Paul, and John all said that this was their favorite song on the album.

"martha My Dear" is a song named after, but not at all about, Paul's sheepdog. George Martin wrote the arrangement for a fourteen-piece orchestra to back Paul, the only Beatle on the track.

john wrote "I'm So Tired" during fits of insomnia at the ashram. A reference to nicotine addiction is made by calling Sir Walter Raleigh a "stupid get."

paul wrote "Blackbird" after reading about the 1968 race riots in the United States. He performed the song solo in the studio, and sound effects of blackbirds, taken from a sound effects album, were overdubbed. Paul claims that he later heard an actual blackbird singing the tune from this song.

george Harrison's mother helped George with "Piggies" by contributing the line about the piggies' needing a whacking. George had worked on various parts of the song since 1966, and didn't feel ready to record until 1968.

paul's inspiration for "Why Don't We Do It in the Road" came from a time in India when he saw two monkeys doing "it" in the road. Paul recorded it almost entirely alone. Without telling any other band members, he laid down the piano, bass, and guitar parts for the song, and the next day had Ringo overdub the drum part. John later expressed annoyance with this solo effort. Paul also recorded "Mother Nature's Son" when the rest of the band was out of the studio.

however, John's only solo song on a Beatles album, "Julia," is on the same album. The song is in the memory of John's mother, and also mentions Yoko Ono by the translation of her name, "ocean child." John's tape-loop composition "Revolution 9" was also done without the other Beatles.

yoko and Patti Harrison contributed backing vocals to the chorus of "Birthday," written by Paul and John while in the studio. Paul recalled coming into the studio at five in the afternoon, and suggesting to John that they just make something up for that evening's session. By the time 9:00 rolled around, they had twenty takes recorded, and by 5:00 A.M. the mono mixing had been finished.

john's "Everybody's Got Something to Hide Except Me and My Monkey" was about his relationship with Yoko, which was under all manner of press scrutiny: "Everybody seemed to be paranoid except for us two, who were in the glow of love."

a "helter skelter" is what the English call the helix-shaped slide that can be found in children's playgrounds. Paul took this slide as an object for his attempt to write the "loudest, nastiest, sweatiest rock number" the Beatles were capable of. One version caught on tape was completely out of control, and went on for over twenty-five minutes. The comment about blisters at the end of the fade-out was a spontaneous remark from Ringo, who actually was bleeding from his hands.

When the book *Helter Skelter*, written by the two prosecutors of the Manson trial, made the bestseller lists in 1976, Capitol Records released the song as a single, with "Got to Get You into My Life" on the A-side. "Helter Skelter" went to number three in the singles charts.

"long, Long, Long" was another George Harrison composition. It was recorded without any input or playing from John.

Although a love song, George insisted in his autobiography, *I Me Mine*, that it was a song for God. He also mentioned that there was a strange unintended sound effect at the end caused by a bottle of Blue Nun wine sitting too close to the organ's amplifier.

"savoy Truffle"** was another Harrison composition, inspired by Eric Clapton's love for chocolates: "At the time he had a lot of cavities in his teeth and needed dental work. He always had toothaches but he ate a lot of chocolates—he couldn't resist them and once he saw a box he *had* to eat them all." The lyrics to the song were taken from a box of "Good News" chocolates, which listed all their varieties: creme tangerine, montelimart, (unlike the song, spelled with an 'r'), ginger sling, etc.

john wrote "Cry Baby Cry," as with "Good Morning," from an advertisement which went "Cry baby cry, make your mother buy."

"revolution 9,"** the famous avant-garde piece composed of overlapping tape loops, was the creation of John, with some help from Yoko. The other members of the band objected to including it on the album, as did George Martin. The voice around which the piece revolves was taken from a studio test tape, which started "This is EMI test series number nine." Other tapes include Paul playing piano, a conversation between John and friend Pete Shotton on LSD, and the fade-out from the single version of "Revolution."

A *Village Voice* poll revealed that "Revolution 9" is the least liked Beatles song. It is also the longest Beatles track—eight minutes, fifteen seconds.

the final track on the White Album is "Good Night," written by John as a lullaby for Julian Lennon, but sung by Ringo. The original conception of Ringo singing while John played acoustic guitar was scrapped for a lavish twenty-six-piece orchestra and an eight-voice choir. "I just said to George Martin," said John, " 'Arrange it like Hollywood. Yeah, corny.' "

"get Back" was the first Beatles song to carry a dual credit: "The Beatles with Billy Preston." Preston, a gospel/rock keyboardist who toured with Little Richard, didn't ask for or expect the credit. Paul took a great deal of criticism for this song, a satire on British immigration policy and ultra-conservative MP Enoch Powell.

the Beatles all share equal credit on "Dig It," which was an in-studio improvisation. The original recording ran to twelve minutes twenty-five seconds, and was edited down heavily for the *Let It Be* album.

john's contribution to Paul's "I've Got a Feeling" was an unfinished song which seemed to fit in the middle of Paul's unfinished composition.

the falsetto voices in the background of the original version of "Across the Universe," singing "Nothing's going to change my world," were provided by two girls Paul met outside the studio, sixteen-year-old Lizzie Bravo from Brazil and seventeen-year-old Gayleen Pease from London. Their voices, along with Paul's backing vocals, were removed from the album version by controversial producer Phil Spector. The Beatles donated the original version for use on the World Wildlife Fund's benefit album *No One's Gonna Change Our World*.

paul wrote "Let It Be" after a dream about his mother, who had been dead for over ten years. In the dream, as Paul told his biographer, she reassured him: "I'm not sure if she used the words 'Let it be' but that was the gist of her advice. . . . I felt very blessed to have that dream. So that got me writing the song 'Let It Be.' I literally started off 'Mother Mary,' which was her name."

"the Ballad of John and Yoko" was the Beatles' first single in stereo. It was written by John as a reaction to the media coverage of his wedding and honeymoon, and displaced "Get Back," which was number one in the British charts. George was out of the country, and Ringo was filming *The Magic Christian*, so John and Paul completed the track alone. Radio stations repeatedly asked Apple to bleep out the reference to Christ, but Apple refused. In the States, the song went to number eight.

throughout "Come Together," John shouted "Shoot me," but only the word "shoot" comes through on the recording. John wrote "Come Together" after his car accident on July 1, 1969.

"something" was George's first and only song to be featured on the A-side of a single. Frank Sinatra remarked that it was "the greatest love song of the past fifty years." Sinatra would, however, during his live performance introduce the song as a Lennon/McCartney composition.

mccartney got the word "pataphysical" for a line in "Maxwell's Silver Hammer" from the French surrealist writer Alfred Jarry. Pataphysics is the "science" of exceptions. Paul was a great fan of Jarry and later surrealists.

Ringo plays an anvil in "Maxwell's Silver Hammer."

John barely concealed his dislike for this song, and took little part in the recording sessions.

ringo was inspired to write "Octopus's Garden" after he left the Beatles temporarily during the White Album sessions. He was on a boat in Sardinia owned by actor Peter Sellers, and was served octopus for lunch. He didn't eat it, but listened to the captain as he explained how octopuses collect and arrange shiny objects in an underwater garden. Ringo sings and also blows air through a straw into a glass of water for this song.

"i Want You (She's So Heavy)" is the longest Beatles song—seven minutes and forty-nine seconds ("Revolution 9" is longer, but few count the tape loop composition as a song.) John said the minimalist song lyrics show Yoko's influence on his writing. John and George over-dubbed guitars repeatedly to get a "heavy metal" sound. Harrison also uses a white noise maker toward the end of the song.

The final mixing for "I Want You" was done on August

20, 1969, the last time all four of the Beatles were in the studio together.

george Harrison wrote "Here Comes the Sun" in spring 1969 in Eric Clapton's garden.

john composed "Because" after hearing Yoko play Beethoven's "Moonlight Sonata" on piano. He asked her to play it backwards, and constructed the melody around what he heard. Paul and George Harrison say this is the best song on *Abbey Road*. George Martin's opinion is that it is the best of all the Beatles' harmonies. John, however, thought it was a "terrible arrangement." It is one of the last Beatles recordings and one of the few latter-day Beatles three-part harmonies.

"you Never Give Me Your Money" was primarily Paul writing about the problems he perceived with Allen Klein's management.

john says he got the idea for "Sun King" from a dream, but at about the same time, Nancy Mitford's biography of Louis XIV, *The Sun King*, had been released to wide reviews.

"polythene Pam" was inspired in John by a woman of a different name who dressed in plastic. "She didn't wear jackboots and kilts," John told *Playboy*, "I just sort of elaborated. Perverted sex in a polythene bag. Just looking for something to write about."

the lyrics to "Golden Slumbers" were from a 1603 song of the same name by Thomas Dekker. The original appears in *The Pleasant Comedy of Old Fortunatus.*

ringo performs the first and only drum solo of his Beatles career on "The End." The other members of the band had to convince him to do it. "I hate solos," said Starr. Paul says he wrote the couplet at the end to follow Shakespeare's tradition of ending his plays with a couplet.

mccartney's solo, acoustic tribute to the Queen of England, "Her Majesty," was not listed on the original album. Paul had instructed that the track be cut out, but the tape operator placed it at the end of the reel, which was normal procedure. The song was mistakenly included on the acetate of *Abbey Road* and Paul found he liked it at the end. The accidental positioning also gives the long silence between "The End" and the start of "Her Majesty," and the barely audible chord with which it starts is actually the fading chord of "Mean Mr. Mustard," revealing the track's original position.

the last Beatle track to be recorded was George Harrison's "I Me Mine," done on January 3, 1970. The original recording was only one minute, thirty-four seconds. Phil Spector's remixing, done in April, extended the track to nearly twice that by simply editing a copy of the song, from where the vocals begin, onto the end. John was not at the session.

following *Beatles for Sale,* released in December 1964, the band recorded only four songs written by others: "Dizzy Miss Lizzy," "Bad Boy," "Act Naturally," and "Maggie Mae."

totaling up their achievements, the Beatles had twenty number one singles on the *Billboard* charts.

the Beatles generally did not listen to their albums after they were finished, and took something of an indifferent attitude toward their songs, as expressed by John in the "official" Beatles biography by Hunter Davies: "It's nice when people like it, but when they start 'appreciating' it, getting great deep things out of it, making a thing of it, then it's a lot of shit.

It proves what we've always thought about most sorts of so-called art. . . . We hated all the shit they wrote and talked about Beethoven and ballet, all kidding themselves it was important. Now it's happening to us. None of it is important. It just takes a few people to get going, and they con themselves into thinking it's important. It all becomes a big con. We're a con as well."

the beatles covered

the first musician to record a Lennon/McCartney composition (besides the Beatles) was Kenny Lynch, who was one of many musicians on the Beatles' first national tour. After "Misery" was rejected by Helen Shapiro's company, he took it on.

"and I Love Her," which appears on *A Hard Day's Night,* proved to be popular with other recording artists—by October 1972, over 370 versions were released.

"can't Buy Me Love" was covered by Ella Fitzgerald, whose version was released shortly after the original. It reached number thirty in the U.K. charts. There are at least seventy other versions of this song.

"all My Loving" has been taken on by nearly 100 other musicians, including Count Basie, Herb Alpert, and the Chipmunks. The song has also been translated into Spanish, French, Portuguese, and Welsh.

fats Domino did a cover of "Everybody's Got Something to Hide Except for Me and My Monkey."

although Paul and John originally wrote "I Wanna Be Your Man," for Ringo, the Rolling Stones recorded a version, and it became their first Top Ten hit.

joe Cocker made his mark covering a Beatles song, "With a Little Help from My Friends."

john performed "I Saw Her Standing There" live with Elton John at Madison Square Garden on November 28, 1974. The performance was released as the B-side to Elton John's "Philadelphia Freedom" in the United States but was an A-side in the United Kingdom.

aerosmith recorded "Come Together" for the *Sgt. Pepper's Lonely Hearts Club Band* film in 1978.

jimi Hendrix covered "Sgt. Pepper's Lonely Hearts Club Band" as his opening number in a concert given just three days after the album's release.

"something" is the second most recorded Beatles song, with over 150 cover versions. James Brown and Smokey Robinson have done versions, and Shirley Bassey's version performed better in the charts than the original.

of all the Beatles' songs, "Yesterday" holds the record for being covered by other musicians. From Frank Sinatra to Marvin Gaye, over 2,500 versions have been recorded.

bibliography

Apple Corps Limited. *The Beatles: A 1997 Year-in-a-Box Calendar*. Indianapolis, IN: Day Dream, Inc., 1996.

Davies, Hunter. *The Beatles*. 2nd revised ed. New York: W. W. Norton & Co., 1996.

Dowlding, William J. *Beatlesongs*. New York: Simon & Schuster, 1989.

Giuliano, Geoffrey. *The Lost Beatles Interviews*. New York: Penguin, 1994.

Harry, Bill. *The Ultimate Beatles Encyclopedia*. New York: Hyperion, 1992.

Hertsgaard, Mark. *A Day in the Life: The Music and Artistry of the Beatles*. New York: Delta/Bantam Doubleday Dell, 1995.

MacDonald, Ian. *Revolution in the Head*. New York: Henry Holt and Company, 1994.

Miles, Barry. *Paul McCartney: Many Years from Now*. New York: Holt, 1997.

Norman, Philip. *Shout! The Beatles in Their Generation*. 2nd Fireside ed. New York: Fireside Books, 1996.

O'Donnell, Jim. *The Day John Met Paul: An Hour-by-Hour Account of How the Beatles Began*. New York: Penguin, 1996.